From Defeat to Victory

by Emily C. Dotson

Companion Press
P.O. Box 310
Shippensburg, PA 17257-0310

"Good Stewards of the
Manifold Grace of God"

ISBN 0-7684-2260-4

For Worldwide Distribution
Printed in the U.S.A.

Acknowledgments

Since my near-death experience with lupus, I give thanks to God for good health. God healed me and He is keeping me well. My story proves that God still heals by the power of stating His Word over bad reports. So I now can show others the way.

I give thanks to Rev. Smith, who prayed for me and sparked my hope when all seemed hopeless. I also give thanks to Dr. Norvel Hayes of Cleveland, Tennessee, for his tape series entitled, "How to Live and Not Die." His tapes taught me how to stand firmly on God's Word until my healing manifested.

I give thanks to Emily Wester of Fuquay Varina, North Carolina for typing and editorial work. Thanks to Patricia Nolan, of Corning, New York, for her editorial work. Thanks also to Eunice Gates of Mount Airy,

North Carolina, and Kay Marlow of Kernersville, North Carolina, for their editorial work. Thanks and God bless Rebecca Reordan also for her typing.

God bless Dorcas Saab of Omaha, Nebraska, for the computer gift so I could finish typing my book. Thanks to Gwen Correll, the late Vince Correll's widow, who assisted with expenses. Thanks to Mr. and Mrs. Bill Boyd, Joanna Micknak and Debbie White also.

And I give thanks to my husband, Jesse, who often prepared meals as I was typing my book. May God bless all who helped with getting my book ready to print!

About the Author

Emily Cornella Dotson and her husband, Jesse, live in King, North Carolina. In her spare time Emily enjoys cooking, gardening, and tending her flowers and watching them grow.

Emily accepted Jesus as her Savior before the age of nine. She was an unhealthy child, and before reaching age 46 she had experienced 11 surgeries for various conditions. After her first back injury in 1979, Emily had liver failure. Then she received her diagnosis: advanced lupus. She is now well and strong from speaking God's Word over her diagnosis until healing manifested.

Emily toured Israel in 1986. While there, she received the baptism of the Holy Spirit and was baptized in the Jordan River. She returned to Israel in November

1991, January 1996, and February 2000. Always when she stepped off the plane she felt that she was on Holy ground, especially so in Jesus' empty tomb.

Dr. Norvel Hayes ordained Emily into the ministry in March 1993. She operates a non-profit organization titled Healing and Restoration Ministries, Inc. She is a missionary evangelist, and teacher, operating from her home in King, North Carolina. Emily is also an executive elder in Dr. Morris Cerullo's ministry.

Emily travels throughout the United States teaching to the terminally ill. She teaches that applying God's Word to problems will halt satanic attacks upon their lives, and that no problem is too big for God to solve as we trust His Word!

Table of Contents

Preface

Emily is a living example of how the Word of God will never return unto Him void. Although Emily was sickly until she reached middle age, she is now well and healthy at the age of 70. She has experienced the power of the spoken Word that brought her healing from many illnesses, including lupus, with both liver and kidney failure.

Emily's life proves that the Holy Spirit continues performing with power as she uses God's Word, demonstrating His Word in her life. By using God's Word and living above sin, she has gained victory over all of satan's attacks.

I have observed Emily's life for many years. She is a proven, faithful servant of God. She is an ordained vessel of His Kingdom. You can be healed as you read her book—that is, if you faithfully apply the healing Scriptures that she used. This is especially true when you continually state God's Word over conditions and circumstances that you are facing in life.

God is no respecter of persons. He will heal you today just as He healed Emily from many illnesses and also from incurable lupus in 1984. But this only applies if you continually execute God's Word, while you stay in faith toward God and His Word! Emily is living proof that God's Word can change your life as it changed her life of defeat to victory!

Rev. Carol Voss

Foreword

From Defeat to Victory extends a desperately needed message to the Body of Christ. Emily's healing ministry has been an extensive and critical part of her message. I met Emily at Gatlinburg Camp Meeting in 1988. She had been diagnosed with lupus and had been given no hope from the doctors.

Although I had not met Emily until 1988, she told me that five years prior, she had purchased my tape series "How To Live and Not Die" when she was near death. She constantly meditated on this series and surrounded herself with God's Word. She continuously confessed, and was miraculously and completely healed from her incurable lupus at the end of 12 months.

Since her miracle, she has been closely connected with me and my ministry. I encourage the reading of this book because it contains a vital message for those who are seeking the victorious life. May you be blessed as you read Emily's experiences. Her message could help make the difference between life and death for you!

Dr. Norvel L Hayes

Chapter 1

Systemic Lupus and My Life Growing Up

I was stunned by a diagnosis of advanced-stage lupus in 1979. At the time I knew little about systemic lupus. Doctors told me that it was incurable. Quickly I set out to learn about this mysterious disease. I found it often disabled its victims. It was located within the metabolism, but was not contagious.

Systemic lupus is unpredictable and debilitating. It is painful and often fatal. The metabolism becomes faulty so that the antibodies turn their attack against the body of the person with lupus. This leaves him or her exhausted. It is as though the body is fighting against itself. Lupus has no known cause and has no medical cure apart from God.

There was no way to predict a given location in my body where lupus would strike, or what specific organ it would damage. Soon I learned more than I wanted to know through painful attacks of lupus. I felt defeated and hopeless. I had not heard of Jesus' being a healer through executing His Word. What a load fell off my mind when I found, at the age of 54, that I could change my world through executing God's Word!

I now relate my life story to prove that no one is too old to change a negative mental image, or to turn their life from defeat to victory by using God's Word. My life is an example that it can be done if you will obey and do what I have done.

Before writing of my serious lupus attacks, I want to take you back into my childhood and inform you of my childhood illnesses. By reading my book you can learn of my strong willpower and how I overcame lupus and other attacks. I beat the odds by using my Bible as a guide, then my faith turned to God's ability! You may draw a conclusion about why lupus struck my body.

Summary of My Childhood

I was born in April 1929, on a family farm near Union Grove, North Carolina, in Iredell County, to Arthur G. and Mamie Call Blankenship. That was the year the stock market crashed. The 1930s followed and were known as the "Great Depression Years."

Those were difficult times for our family. I was the youngest of seven children. Though the firstborn died soon after birth, the six remaining siblings crowded our home and strained the family budget, thus creating financial hardship.

When my parents married, they were both teaching in a small rural school district, with a four or five-month teaching term in the 1920s. Salaries were low, so, as our family grew, both parents stopped teaching. Daddy farmed full-time and worked a garden to feed us. Mother had many pregnancies and many illnesses. When I was born, she was 40 and very frail.

When I was three, Mother was physically ill and emotionally exhausted. She went to her parents' home for rest and never returned. Because I was barely three, I do not remember her nurturing me as a daughter. Dad acted as both father and mother; he never remarried, but stayed close by as a strict God-fearing father. He taught good principles and read the Bible to us, but I was lonely without a mother's love and I missed her nurturing.

My sisters Fay and Lucy and Dad took care of me. I felt safe as Dad was strong and I was small and frail. Dad was a Christian who never let us skip church unless we were too ill to attend. Our church was an old-time denominational church. The ladies shouted and ran the aisles, praising God. The pastor taught of Jesus as Savior and he really loved God, but never taught us to execute healing Scriptures. Not knowing to speak God's Word only, I was slow finding Jesus as healer and I remained sickly.

I felt close to Daddy since Mother was gone. Dad tried to take Mother's place but that was impossible. Every girl needs a mother's love and her close relationship. When I was small I daydreamed of having a mother holding and loving me.

My sister Mary and my brother Charles were both older than I was. Charles played with marbles and Mary read books. They never played with me so I had to play alone most of the time.

We all worked hard growing up on a small farm. Cotton was our only money crop. Picking cotton was a backbreaking job. In those days, there were no machines to pick the cotton so we did it by hand. The price of cotton was three cents a pound because of the Great Depression in the 1930s, so finances were low. It was difficult to have enough income to cover all our family expenses.

We raised corn and wheat that Daddy hauled by horse and wagon to a roller mill four miles away. There the grains were ground into cornmeal or flour for bread, or feed for our animals. It took a lot of grain for the cows, pigs, chickens and horses. Our family of seven, plus all the animals, had to be fed.

We worked hard as Dad allowed none to be lazy. There were gardens to weed and cotton and corn to hoe. We each had chore assignments. In the summers, we canned food for the next winter. We ate no dainty food, only fruit and vegetables from the garden. Dad taught that if we failed to work we could not eat. Hard work never killed us, although as children we thought it would.

When I was a child in the 1930s, we had no automobile for transportation. We walked or used a horse and buggy. I remember riding in a horse drawn buggy one cold winter day as Daddy took my sister Fay to a doctor. Dad wrapped us in a heavy woolen blanket to keep the icy-cold air from freezing us. Although our faces were cold, our bodies were cozy and warm.

There were no cars on the dirt road to spook Bob our horse, so he felt safe. I can recall seeing the first automobile drive down our dirt road. That car scared our chickens half to death. They ran screaming toward the barn for cover and safety.

Although I was sickly, my health improved each summer when I worked in the fields, fresh air, and sunshine. But when winter came, I would become very sickly. Our farmhouse was cold and hard to heat, so it was difficult to avoid being chilled. I had allergies, poor health, and constant attacks of illness. It really seemed that satan's strategy was to destroy me from infancy.

Each time I got chilled I contracted laryngitis, tonsillitis or pneumonia. I seldom played outside in the winter. There were nights I would awaken, gasping and choking with what was called old-time croup. Many children back in those days died with that kind of croup before reaching medical help. We could not afford medical help, so Daddy prayed and used household remedies that always worked, and I would survive each attack.

I remember one cold night when I was small that I awoke around 4:00 a.m., choking and struggling for breath. I felt I was dying; I could scarcely breathe. I stumbled to Dad's bedside, unable to speak. I was shivering with cold. I only made a strange, squeaky, hoarse sound from my throat like a frog.

Daddy jumped out of bed, threw a blanket around me, ran to the fireplace, and stirred the ashes to find live fire coals. He found a few live ones, then he quickly ran to the kitchen to get a tablespoon of cold pork lard. He put the spoon down on the live fire coals until the lard was melted. After testing the temperature with his finger, he poured the contents of the spoon down my throat. In seconds I could breathe freely, and satan's plan to kill me was stopped by Daddy's quick actions.

I recall an accident that happened when I was three and a half, and my brother, Charles, was six. It was on a cold winter day when Dad had taken grain to the roller mill to be ground into flour for bread and feed for the animals. He left our sister Fay in charge. When she became interested in reading a book, Charles and I put our coats on and ran outside.

Once outside, Charles told me of his plan to cross the wide creek and get walnuts. I said I was going also. He told me I couldn't, but I tagged along. I followed him and we ran fast as we could down the hill into the woods, toward the swift water. Large rocks lay across the creek to pond up the water and make a dam. We had crossed there before with older siblings, but we were too young to be aware of any danger by crossing alone. Our thoughts were not on danger, but on gathering walnuts to eat.

Charles was strong for his age, but neither of us could swim. After carefully crossing over the dam, we reached the walnut tree. My brother filled his pockets and arms with walnuts, and I quickly filled my lap. He said we must work fast and get back before Fay found out we were gone. She must not know that we had disobeyed Daddy's rule not to cross the water without an adult. Children will take big chances when no one is watching them, and we were no exception. Our desire for walnuts drove us there, so quickly we gathered them.

Then, as fast as our short legs would carry us, we hurried back toward the creek. As we reached the creek bank, Charles told me to be careful and keep my balance as I walked the slick rocks. I assured him that I would. My lap was full of walnuts and I never realized that I could not see where my feet stepped.

I was proud of my ability to follow my brother's footsteps. I tried to be careful. My concern was that if my feet slid I would fall into the icy water. I never realized that I might drown. So I carefully walked the slick rocks on the dam, until I reached the middle of the creek.

Then it happened. Suddenly my feet slipped and down I fell into icy-cold, swift water. I screamed to my brother, "Help, help!" He dropped his armful of walnuts and stood on the dam. Reaching down, he took my extended hand. With my other hand I held onto a rock on the dam to keep the water from carrying me away. Quickly, he pulled me to safety.

My walnuts were gone and so were the ones Charles held in his arms. He was angry that I had tagged along and spoiled his adventure. It's a miracle we didn't drown. We were wet, chilled, half-frozen, and shivering when we reached home. We never told Dad, for if he had known he would have punished Fay for not watching us more closely. Fay stripped our wet clothing. She built a big fire in the fireplace, drying us quickly so we would not catch pneumonia. Later on, the exposure did cause allergies.

That same year, my sister Lucy made me a teddy bear from fuzzy scrap cloth. He was my only stuffed animal. I named him Teddy and he was my security blanket. I hugged and played with him until one day Teddy was missing. I was heartbroken. My brother

Charles knew how much I loved Teddy, but he confessed that once when he was angry with me, he had buried beloved Teddy.

Later Mother mailed a store-bought doll to me and I was so delighted. I named her Rose and played with her for hours. I was so happy to have a beautiful new doll. It was the only doll that I ever had, and it was the only store-bought doll that was ever in our home. My doll Rose comforted me and helped me to forget my grief over the loss of my teddy bear.

Time passed quickly and just before I turned nine, satan tried to take my life again. This attack came in the form of German measles. I came down with them in February when it was very cold in our home that had only one fireplace. There was not one spot on me that was not covered with measles. My fever ran high, and I almost dehydrated. We had no money to pay a doctor and no car for transportation. I lay unconscious for three days.

When I regained consciousness, I saw a vision with my eyes wide open. I was not dreaming. The wall vanished away and I saw into the flames of hell. It appeared the people in the red flames were struggling, trying to escape. The flames rose up, then went down and rose up again, as the people in the flames seemed to be tormented. I knew that it was hell as Dad had read about hell from the Bible. I had also heard about hell at church.

I was very frightened, and I screamed loudly. My sister Fay ran to my bedside and asked what was wrong. I told her what I saw, but she saw nothing. I knew then that she thought I was delirious. However, I knew that I had seen a vision of hell. I thought that since she did not see hell, no one else would believe me either. So, I just kept the vision of hell buried within my memory and never told another soul.

That vision always remained fresh on my mind. If I live to be one hundred, I will not forget that vision. I knew that I needed to be saved. I knew that if I died that I would go into those flames unless I took Jesus as my Savior. But I did not know how to get saved at that time.

Pneumonia followed the measles. I lay sick for weeks as satan tried to snuff out my life. My attack came before antibiotics were discovered and at a time when many died of pneumonia. But Daddy's prayers were more powerful than any doctors' medicine! Miraculously, I survived without antibiotics.

I remember Daddy kneeling by my bedside praying silently as I drifted in and out of consciousness. His prayers pulled me through satan's attacks of both measles and pneumonia. I slowly regained strength, with no antibiotics, no aspirin, and no doctor. God surely kept me alive for some specific purpose!

I began to improve slowly as winter passed and spring came. It was good to have warm weather so I could get out of the house and run and play again. I felt like a bird out of its cage. I was happy and free, running and playing in the fields and woods in the sunshine, after my long winter illness.

Then springtime ended, summer followed, and the vision of hell still haunted my mind. I prayed that God would not let me die and go there. I needed to be born again. Yet no one knew that I was at the age of accountability. At that time, I never told anyone of the turmoil in my soul or of what was on my mind.

Two months after my vision of hell, I turned nine years old. The vision haunted me for four more months until our annual church revival in August 1938. Kneeling at our church altar, I asked Jesus to come into my heart and be my Savior. I knew that something great had happened as the weight of fear lifted.

I did not fully understand my new experience. I only knew that I felt light as a feather. All condemnation lifted off my soul and my fear of dying and going to hell vanished. I never feared death again, though I have had some near-death experiences. Each time I escaped death and survived.

Each spring my health improved, and I enjoyed playing outside. I had no close neighbors to play with, so when cousins came I enjoyed their visits and looked forward to their coming. In the summers I enjoyed playing ball outside with my cousins.

When the winter snows fell my brothers and sisters played in the beautiful snow, as I watched from my window. I longed to go out and play with them, but seldom was I allowed to. So I played inside with my doll, Rose, because if I got chilled I got sick.

Daddy kept me occupied by reading Bible stories of great heroes. My favorite ones were about Joseph and David. They both spent much time alone with God, just as I did. Also I heard of Jesus the Savior, but was taught little about Jesus as my Healer, so I stayed in bondage to illness. Hearing the Word kept me from becoming restless while confined in the house.

Each year as spring came and warm breezes blew, I took long walks and picked wildflowers in the woods and fields on the backside of our small farm. I loved God's creation very much. I watched the birds fly and squirrels scamper up the tall trees.

Once I found a nest of baby opossums that had been abandoned by their mother. I carried the five baby opossums home for my brother Paul to feed. He fed them daily with a thin liquid of cornbread and milk. Soon they began to grow larger. Then while I was visiting Lucy, my married sister, my brother turned the opossums loose into the woods. When I returned home I was sad because they were gone. Paul said they were not happy inside the cage, and I realized they were happier running free.

Soon I forgot about the opossums because I had other animals to play with. I was truly an animal lover. Someone once told me that if a boy loved animals, he would be good to his wife. This may be true because if he mistreated animals, he may also mistreat his wife. I loved animals and would never mistreat one of them.

Once a stray dog attacked one of our chickens, and she lay helpless and bleeding. I picked her up and put medicated salve over her exposed intestines. I wrapped her in gauze bandages and placed her inside a chicken coop. I never wanted animals to suffer so I took care of her daily. Soon she recovered and followed after me like a little pet puppy.

In the 1930s most people living on farms were poor, so we never realized how poor we were. We were thankful to have pretty clothes made of floral, printed feed sacks that had once contained feed for our cows. When the sacks were emptied, they were made into pretty dresses. We each had two pretty dresses. I kept my dresses clean by washing them daily. In the winter, I hung them by the fireplace to dry so they would be clean for school the next day. I loved school but I was absent much with illness.

After school I ran in the woods, and picked wildflowers and berries after chores were done. I walked along, talking to Jesus as He walked with me. He was my best friend. I began to build a relationship with Him. Though I missed a relationship with Mother, I no longer felt lonely because Jesus' Spirit had moved in with me. He filled the void by taking Mother's place.

When I was a child it was hard to understand Dad's strict rules. We thought they were too tough. If we broke his rules, he gave us a big whipping. But I loved him enough that I would have laid my life down for him as he lay dying near the age of 87.

If a child is not taught obedience at home he never honors his parents, nor does he honor God! Obedience instills honor and reverence in children. We may not agree with our parents' rules, but that's no ground for disobedience. (See Ephesians 6:1.)

God used my experiences as tools to draw me into a closer relationship with Him. My disappointments, heartaches, sorrows, and illnesses have all reshaped and molded me into a more sympathetic person with a concern for the suffering ones.

It was painful to my flesh as God molded and re-shaped me, yet it was necessary. My experiences helped me build a closer relationship with God. He was preparing me as His vessel. However, back then I was unaware of His purpose.

When I was a sickly 12-year-old, my 18-year-old sister Mary got a job, leaving me to cook and clean house for Dad and my brothers. We had no electricity, washing machine, or dryer, no television or telephone. I worked hard washing clothes on a tin washboard, doing cooking and housecleaning. But each night after meals, we enjoyed hearing the Grand Old Opry on our battery-powered radio. Each night, Daddy and I would sing along.

When I was 15, my two brothers went off to serve in World War II. Our crops were left in the fields for Dad and me to harvest. We had chickens, pigs, and a horse to feed as well as cows to milk. That truly was a difficult year for both Dad and me. I had to quit school to help Dad gather the crops from the fields. We both worked late every night. I was sick and exhausted by the time the corn and cotton crops were gathered from the fields. It was Christmastime when all our tasks were finished.

I cooked and did housework, fieldwork, and wrote letters to my brothers in the army. Being the last child to leave home, I dreaded to leave Dad alone, but knew that at 18 I would have to go. There was little income from our small farm.

I was a sickly, sheltered, shy young lady as I turned 18. Dad was then in his sixties. At that time my oldest sister's husband went away to war, so she came home to live. That settled the issue for me about leaving Dad alone. I felt free to go.

I was ready to leave the nest and start my new life. Although I was sickly and shy, I had an adventurous spirit with no fear of the future. I knew Jesus was holding my future in His hands. So in 1947 at age 18, I left the home where I grew up at Union Grove, North Carolina.

I had no car at that time, so daily I rode the bus to my place of employment in Winston-Salem, North Carolina. The city was 50 miles from where I grew up in Iredell County. I could not visit Daddy back home very often, because the bus was my only transportation. But my adventurous spirit drove me on. Without any fear of my future I started my new life out on my own.

Chapter 2

Departing Home and Getting Married

Moving from the country into the city was quite an adjustment for me. I had to change from a lifestyle of hard work on the farm to a fast-paced city routine. I once heard it said that you can take someone out of the country, but you can never take the country out of him or her. I believe that saying could be true. I dug up my backyard with a mattock and shovel, and planted a vegetable and flower garden in the city!

Daily, after my public job ended, I worked in my vegetable and flower garden. I was not lazy, and my country lifestyle of hard work remained. Staying busy kept loneliness from my mind as I adjusted to the city life.

Dad never allowed me to date before I was 18. He warned me of wolves in sheep's clothing. Back then I never knew the importance of his warning. I was well disciplined; I worked on a farm and went to church with Daddy. I knew nothing of a worldly lifestyle. I had no idea what city life was like. What a shock I got meeting some city girls and observing their loose lifestyle!

In the city I often felt lonely, yet I was never afraid of anything. Although I was sickly, Jesus was my protection and I knew His presence kept me safely. My relationship with Him kept me from falling into satan's deceitful, destructive fear trap.

I took a room in town at a boarding house where other girls lived. At the week's end, my paycheck barely covered expenses for room and board. Though I had little money, my attitude and outlook were so different from those of the other girls.

Every day I awakened singing cheerfully, because I had a joyful heart even though my body was sickly. The other girls awoke with a headache and a hangover, asking why I sang when my feet hit the floor. I sang because I was happy that I was saved. They never appreciated my songs that I sang to the Lord.

The girls joked, whispering and saying that I was too sanctified to listen. I appreciated their respect as I never wanted to hear dirty jokes. I knew that Jesus did not want me to hear their jokes because His Spirit lived within my spirit.

I soon felt a division that came from being a Christian in a sinful world. The girls shunned me until things went wrong for them. Then they wanted my prayer, without my fellowship, just as they wanted God's blessings without fellowshiping with Him. But we must always seek God's face before we seek His helping hand!

Since I was away from home and knew so few people, I was lonely for fellowship. I loved people and had no problem making friends. My dilemma was that these girls were not Christians; we had little in common. They knew I loved God, so their loose lifestyle made them feel uncomfortable in my presence. I had no place to go but to God. I wanted their acceptance, but was determined not to backslide and live in sin to be accepted.

There may be pleasure in sin for a season, yet I wanted no part of that lifestyle. I loved Jesus and had been taught better. I feared losing His fellowship as He was my best friend. My life was built around Jesus. When I was lonely, I talked to Him.

Although I was sickly, I never acted as though I was frail. I was cheerful and happy so the boys often asked me for a date. Most times I declined and went bowling with the girls instead. I was far more interested in pleasing the Lord.

I remained true to God and never backslid. I stayed calm when the other girls at the boarding house got upset. They never understood that my relationship with God kept me at peace. I was settled and never acted wild as most teenagers do.

Although I had constant health attacks, no doctor diagnosed me with lupus back then. I searched for answers to all my health problems, hoping that someone could help me. But I never found sufficient knowledge to get healed. I needed someone to teach me healing faith from God's Word, as healing faith only comes from hearing God's healing Scriptures from the Bible.

One denominational church told me that healing had passed away with the apostles. Not all denominational churches teach that, but the one I attended did. Incorrect teaching kept me from receiving my healing for years, so satan kept me in bondage with sickness.

It is a shame that most pastors never teach the sins of health neglect, yet they teach not to commit sins of stealing, lying, and adultery. Our bodies are temples that God's Spirit dwells within. It's sin to mistreat or neglect our health care.

Since I was reared without a mother, I had no one to teach me to eat properly in order to gain good health. And when I went out on my own, I did not have the money to buy nutritious food and vitamins. I was a prime target for satan's attacks because of my allergies, poor health, and poor eating habits.

If satan cannot make us fall into sin, he then attacks our bodies when our resistance is low. In another chapter, I teach and stress correct eating habits. But for now, I want to say that God expects certain things of us. He expects us to rest, strive to keep His laws, eat properly, and care for our bodies.

God chooses our birthplace and also our parents. He is in control of our lives, yet He gives us a choice as to how we want to live our life. He does not control our wills. He allows us a will to choose whether to serve Him, or not to serve or obey.

We may destroy our bodies if we choose, but it's not God's will. "Beloved, I pray that you may prosper in all things and be in health..." (3 John 2). Our soul must prosper before our health can prosper, as all healing begins in the soulish realm.

God has since taught me proper eating habits. He gave me a desire to study nutrition and to learn proper healthcare. I was eager to learn so that I could get well. I desired to be healthy so that satan could not destroy my body with so many attacks.

Also, we must be aware of how satan moves people in our path to hinder our walk with God. We must learn of his schemes or we may take offense at those he works through. Often, satan goes undetected as the villain causing those offenses, and then we get upset at people instead of him. (See Ephesians 6:10-18.)

We must walk in love or we grow bitter. God wants us to be His love vessels. He is the potter; I am His clay vessel. He has molded on me for 70 years, and He is not finished with me yet!

Back then it was difficult holding a job. I had many allergies and health attacks from satan. I got the flu every winter and often had bronchitis and pneumonia. On and on the attacks went, and although it was tough, I continued working.

Most people would have grown weary, given up hope, and said "forget it" after all the struggles. Yet I knew deep within me that my life had a purpose, and I wanted to fulfill it. Dear reader, if you are sick or have a bad report from a doctor, I urge you to keep reading, and you will surely find your answer.

I'm relating many painful details of satan's attacks, with the hope that it may keep you from pitfalls that I encountered although I was a Christian. If you keep reading, you will see the depth to which satan will go to try to destroy one of God's children. Know this, too, that by using God's Word as a sword, you can take yourself out of defeat and move on into victory!

We must learn God's Word, because God never blesses ignorance. Satan inflicts curses from our lack of knowing or applying God's Word. (See Deuteronomy 30:19 or Hosea 4:6.) We must seek knowledge from God's Word and not remain in spiritual ignorance. Choose life and seek healing God's way from His Word.

Remaining ignorant allows satanic attacks, while God could have blessed us through the wisdom that comes by using His Word. Some say wisdom is acquired by age, but that is not always true. I know some elderly ones who have no wisdom. Wisdom is gained by knowing God intimately. It has taken me a lifetime to learn how to live in victory; and that's only by exercising God's wisdom principles from His Word. I'm now 70 and I am still learning.

God watched to see how much I exercised my faith. When I was a baby, my muscles were weak until I used them. I stood, I crawled, I walked, I fell down, and I got up and tried again. My faith walk worked the same way. As my faith fell down from sickness and trials, I got up and tried again. God helped me each time. My experiences made me grow stronger as He kept chiseling off my rough edges to make me His vessel.

God allowed me to endure fiery trials when I was in the refining process. He was teaching and training me to trust and depend on Him. My relationship with God kept satan from destroying me, though he tried many times. He made attempts to kill me on the highways. Sometimes I lost control of my car on ice, and sometimes I skidded on rain-slick roads. I would say, "Oh Jesus, help me," and He would take control of my car.

When I accepted Jesus as my Savior, I became subject to Heaven's authority. God wanted me to learn not to judge things by my feelings but to judge by what His Word said. It took years to learn my lesson, but once I learned that fact and put it in action, I was on the right road. God's Word was my answer. I cannot live by bread only; I live by His Word also. (See Luke 4:4).

Each time I climbed one mountain, it seemed the next one got higher. Climbing over my trials exercised my faith. So I got lots of practice. God was building faith muscles and teaching me to depend on His promises instead of depending on others. People can fail us, but God never will! He wants us to trust Him in every trial as the apostle Paul did. As Paul looked to Jesus while running his faith race, so must I as I run mine. I intend to run my race to the finish line no matter how difficult it may be.

When I was growing up, Daddy never allowed me to go places where drinking or dancing were practiced. I will always be grateful for his protection and strict training. He protected and guarded us closely, just as God also has protected and kept me from situations others may have experienced. I have never been molested or raped. I have not lived a sinful life by drinking, adultery, gambling, doing dope, or going to clubs. I loved the things of the Lord and was hungry for His presence.

I loved going to church and hearing about Jesus. I had no association with worldly people. I was ignorant of that lifestyle and had no desire to know about it. Growing up, my goal was to marry a preacher like my Uncle Glenn. (Incidentally, I missed my goal of marrying a preacher.)

Trusting people was easy for me, as I had learned to trust Dad as well as my Heavenly Father. I learned that both my dad and my Heavenly Father were trustworthy. I never knew distrust as a child. I was taught honesty and thought most people were honest. If I had been baptized in the Holy Spirit then, I may have had wisdom enough to not trust the man that I married.

I never fully believed what Dad said about wolves in sheep's clothing until a wolf caught me. I did not know how to look for a husband by looking for the fruit of the Spirit. So I got stuck with a wolf calling himself a Christian! Now I know the fruit of the Spirit that's listed in Galatians 5:22-23: "But the fruit of the Spirit is love, joy, peace, long-suffering, kindness, goodness, faithfulness, gentleness, self-control. Against such there is no law."

I never knew to look for those qualities when I married. I could have been spared many heartaches and sorrows. Take my advice; never plan to marry a person who does not have all the qualities that I just mentioned. Drop him or her like a hot potato. You cannot change a person. And God cannot override their will! Life is unbearable until your spouse's character changes, and he or she may never change. That mate must be willing and have a desire to be changed by God.

Some things we may experience are just as bad as molestation or rape. Those things are physical abuse, slander, mental abuse, and bondage to a husband filled with a demon of hate and rage. Those things eat away at your heart and soul, sapping your joy. Satan used those tools in my life to steal my joy with the intention of destroying my walk with Jesus. Satan cleverly motivates people who are without a relationship with God.

My joy was gone before I learned that human flesh was not my problem. Spiritual wickedness was my enemy. I believe that satan had me marked for destruction from birth. The evil spirit realm is very real and can overpower us unless we learn to stand on God's Word. God's Word is much more powerful than the satanic spirit realm that works against us. However, back then I never knew how to use the authority of God's Spiritual Word on satan.

It is so important to go to a church that teaches us how to use the authority of God's Word on the enemy so that he does not beat us down. There were no good Spirit-filled churches near me teaching the authority God's Word carries. How was I to learn if I was not taught? Most churches were afraid to even mention the devil's name. At my church no one taught how to win over satanic attacks. My ignorance caused him to attack me often.

I would not have suffered through all that I endured by the enemy if I had been taught the spiritual authority that I have as a born-again believer of God. The devil took advantage of my ignorance, just as he takes advantage of our ignorance from saying wrong words. I never knew to proclaim the health that I needed so I just repeated my sickness and sorrows. I know now, though, to proclaim the good that I need and refuse the bad!

The purpose of a trial is to prove our faith and make us grow stronger. I truly have had my share of testing and trials to prove my faith, but God always stood faithfully with me. My physical attacks only made the fight in my spirit become greater and drove me closer to God. There was no other place that I could go! God was the only one who could heal my soul and body.

I am happy that I learned the truth of God's Word before I went to my grave. I would have gone to Heaven without fearing death. But I never would have known the joy of speaking and using God's Word to heal my body. Neither could I have taught others to stand on the Word for their healing. Now I am happy knowing that Jesus will give me a crown for overcoming!

God is a loving Father who desires fellowship far more than lip service or memorizing or quoting His Word to impress others. And God watches to see how much of His Word we will obey.

We also must learn not to continually repeat and speak the bad things that happen to us. Instead, we must verbally thank God that things are changing, and then He will change them. If I had known sooner that I could have had what I said, I would have been spared much pain and sorrow. I never knew that I should say what I needed. Instead, I stated the misery that I had! I finally found that when I repeated it, I kept it! So if you want to change circumstances and conditions, then change your words!

A baby Christian must learn to exercise his faith like a muscle. That way, his faith can grow stronger just as his physical muscles grow stronger by using them. I have exercised my faith this way, and God has been so patient with me as I learned.

Although I had one illness after another, I still managed to keep my job so I could pay my doctor bills. It was difficult to work since I was sick so often. I would get over one attack and then have to fight another. I never would have survived if Jesus had not been with me in my fiery trials. Jesus was my companion, so I stayed cheerful and my sickness never defeated my spirit.

My health did improve somewhat, and as I turned 19, I met a young man with whom I worked. He asked me out on a date. Before consenting, I asked if he was a Christian and he said that he was. So I believed him. It never occurred to me that he was deceptive because he treated me so nicely. So we went out bowling and he behaved like a gentleman.

We dated, fell in love, and were married in May 1950. He was 27 and I had just turned 21. Sixteen months later we had our first daughter. Three years later we had our second daughter. We had two lovely daughters by the time I was 25. After my first child's birth, my physical problems started again.

My health declined steadily. I had kidney poisoning when my first child was three months old. I lay for weeks at the point of death before recovering from that attack. My doctor came to our home and gave me a large shot of penicillin, which caused an allergic reaction that almost took my life.

My doctor came back to give me shots to counteract the penicillin. He told me not to take penicillin again as it could kill me. I was swollen all over and in pain. After that attack, I used Mycin drugs for the infections that came frequently thereafter.

When our children were small, it was difficult for me to care for them. I was sickly, and my husband had no thought of helping with the housework, washing, cooking, or canning. His patience was short, so his temper was always hot and extremely explosive.

His anger often exploded on me, or he beat our youngest daughter, who had bronchial asthma until she was seven. In 1961 I took her to a Dr. Oral Roberts meeting in Charlotte, North Carolina. We braved a cold rain for hours to get into the building. Rain usually caused her asthma attacks. But healing came instantly and asthma never returned in the 38 years since then. Thanks to God and thanks to Dr. Roberts.

Once, when the children were small and my spirit was low, I got a letter from my elderly dad. Inside his letter was a small booklet by Dr. Oral Roberts entitled, "Holding the Rope." It touched my aching heart, and I cried for hours after reading it.

That little booklet touched my life tremendously. I knew that Daddy surely felt my discouragement. Once he told me I could come home if I needed to. I never told him how I was mistreated, but he sensed things were bad. My cheerful and joyful nature was gone; I was often tearful instead.

I have kept the small booklet that Daddy sent me more than 40 years ago, although it has turned yellow with age. Neither Daddy nor Dr. Oral Roberts may know, this side of Heaven, all the encouragement that booklet gave to me. It came on a dreary winter day when I had almost lost hope of my deliverance from the horrible pit and danger that I faced daily!

In the booklet Dr. Roberts said to hold onto the rope for someone, that the life you hold at the end of the rope might be in danger. He told how the early Christians had let the apostle Paul down outside the city wall of Jerusalem in a basket by a rope. He said that by their deed, they had saved his life.

Neither Daddy nor Dr. Roberts ever knew that I was the one whose life was in danger, or that I was the one at the end of the rope that day. I am thankful that Dr. Oral Roberts wrote the small booklet many years ago. It gave me courage to know that someone was holding my rope. I am thankful Dad mailed the booklet at such a crucial time, and that he "held my rope" for me.

My health was at its breaking point from my unhappiness and the abuse. All of it had taken a toll on me. Misery and unhappiness are both vicious killers and satan is the author of both. He came to steal, to kill, and to destroy. (See John 10:10). I was a prime target without knowing his plans were to kill me.

Again Dad asked me to come home, but my husband said if I left he would not support us. He also said that he would take the girls away from me. Then he said that if I left he would kill himself. That was his way of keeping me in his abusive control. My health was too poor to resume sole support of the girls. I felt trapped and so in need of help, hanging at the end of my rope!

I clung to Dr. Oral Roberts' small booklet and to my Bible. Both gave me comfort. Thank God my husband never took my Bible from me, as it never cost him anything. Rev. Jack Johnson of Mount Airy, North Carolina, to whom I listened on WPAQ radio, had sent me the Bible. I read it daily, and wondered if God would ever deliver me from the misery and danger that I continually faced.

I wondered if I would ever have a normal happy life. I prayed for my husband and clung to hope that he would change. I filled my pillow with tears nightly. Then hope began to fade after 15 years passed and his abuse only became worse each year.

My health rapidly declined; I knew a solution must come soon if I were to survive. Something had to change so I could live to rear our two precious daughters. Hope in God was all I had to cling to!

Chapter 3

Life Endangered, a Warning, and a Night Vision

I recall having the dreadful Asian flu three times in 1959. I spent most of that bitter cold winter in bed with fever and chills. Our two young girls were in school, and my husband was working. I got out of bed to cook meals only by using sheer willpower. I survived and was glad to see spring come that year.

My health steadily declined after those three attacks of the Asian flu, and I began having migraine headaches. The doctor made x-rays of both my sinuses and brain, hoping to find the cause of the migraines. The cause was not found at that time, so from 1959 to 1970, I continued to suffer with the headaches.

Meanwhile, I developed an ulcer that ate through my colon. Dr. Howard Starling in Winston-Salem, North

Carolina, said I must have surgery at once as he thought I had cancer. My elderly dad was alive then. He drove 50 miles to pray for me. After he prayed, my infection left, but the hole remained until surgery.

Though Dr. Starling said he felt I had cancer, my husband would not allow surgery for four months. There was no insurance to pay my hospital bill. My husband treated me cruelly, saying that he hoped I would die. Dad was heartbroken over my problem. My sister tried to convince my doctor to operate without my husband's consent. He declined, fearing a lawsuit.

My husband never helped me with housework when the girls were small, and that placed undue stress on me because of my frail condition. By the time the surgeon removed six inches of my colon, my recovery was slow. My surgeon said I had escaped cancer by a thread. Surely Daddy's prayers kept me from having cancer.

If I had not known the Lord, I never could have survived what I endured. My husband's temper always flared at the most frivolous things done by our daughters or me. Usually I was the target of his fury, but at times he vented his fury on our younger daughter also. The two girls and I tolerated much more than we ever should have, because of his violent temper.

He yelled and often abused me with his fists. I thought a divorce was wrong, so I tried to make the best of it and hold on. There seemed no solution. I was ashamed to tell anyone of my abuse, just as other women also want their abuse kept secret.

My husband's parents were sad at the bad way we were treated. They tried to talk to him, but his temper flared and he cursed them. He was jealous because he thought they loved me more than they loved him. I lived with his cruelty for 15 years.

Many times during 15 years, he left me at home alone at night with our two small daughters while he went out. On Saturday nights he bathed, dressed in his best suit and left, returning after midnight. Then I would hear water running again, as he took his second shower. I knew never to ask where he had been. If I had asked where he had been his anger would have flared into rage, as it had flared before. Then he would have abused me.

I was hopelessly trapped with no way out. I tried to stay out of his way, and that was like walking on thin ice. I never knew when he would explode, so I never could relax. I thought that perhaps his problems might be related to a time when he was shell-shocked in World War II, as his nerves were in shambles. He often managed to make me feel sorry for him.

When in a good mood, he would say he knew I was the best wife in the world. But he was seldom in a good mood. At times, he would say that he did not know why he often mistreated me. Then he would say no one loved him but me. I knew his mother and daddy loved him, yet he was jealous because they also loved me. He did not want his family to love or fellowship with me, but they loved me anyway. Even forty years later his anger flared when I was invited to attend his mother's funeral.

At times he would hit me with his fist, then jump in his car and leave, so he would not see me cry and feel guilty. I would run to our den and fall on my knees, crying out for God's help, so I would not hate him. I knew if hate got in my heart, that satan had permission to attack. As I cried to God, the hurt and pain would leave my heart, so I could endure another day.

Once my husband saw a scratch on the kitchen cabinet door and flew into a rage. He came at me with a butcher knife. I ran into the woods and stayed there until midnight when the house was dark. Then I returned, feeling that he was surely fast asleep.

Another time he grabbed me by the throat and started choking me. I could see the two small girls at the edge of the hallway, looking on in horror. As I felt my breath leaving, I reached for his glasses. He stiffened his arms and pushed me farther away. He tightened his grip on my throat and began choking me. I knew that I must live for the sake of my two small daughters.

With all my strength I reached out further for his glasses. Quickly, I pulled them off his face. I knew that this action would stop his attack, as he already had a hard time adjusting his glasses so they did not hurt his nose. Instantly, he let go of my throat and started to cry and whimper like a little puppy. I was safe then, until the next time his anger flared and he exploded.

Once I rode to work with a friend. She came for a visit and brought her two small children. She did not know that my husband would at times fly into a rage. He took her small son and shook him violently, yelling at him as he began to drag a small chair, making a small scratch on our shiny hardwood floor. My friend never returned, nor did any other friend, because of my husband's temper.

My pastor knew of my physical abuse and said that I should leave my husband, as God never wanted anyone mistreated like that. He also said that I could never marry again, though he was unaware of my husband's unfaithfulness.

I asked my pastor if my husband had demons. His reply was that there are no demons now—that only occurred in Bible days. I wish a pastor with that mentality could follow me now and watch as I cast demons out. Demons can hide in people and do violent and weird things, keeping them in bondage until they get deliverance. A person who is possessed is even capable of committing murder, yet he may not realize that he did it, until he regains control of his senses. He may even be unaware that it was a demon that influenced him to do the evil deed.

If God had not delivered me from my husband's abuse, I could have been badly harmed. I had no knowledge how to protect myself from an evil spirit then. I was unaware that my abuse came because satan hated me and wanted to destroy me. Finally God gave a dream stating I must escape. As I obeyed, God spared my life.

A wife must be cautious if her husband is unfaithful and physically abusive. I cannot tell others to do as I did, rather to seek God's advice! I know what God told me in my situation. He warned me that my life was in danger, yet I hesitated to go. I never wanted a divorce, nor did my church approve of divorce.

I cannot criticize that belief, only that my pastor could not cast a demon out. If he had cast the demon out of him, we may not have divorced. He was controlled by a demon of rage; however, he thought he was in control. At times he would say he wondered why he acted as badly as he did when he got angry.

Many nights as I lay sleeping, my husband would come home late and kick me from bed onto the floor. He would curse and say I belonged on the floor. I'm writing my book for those in similar bondage. There is hope for you! After 15 years of his abuse, God delivered me! He will do the same for you if you trust Him.

According to my husband's jealous thinking, I loved God more than I loved him, so he was angry about my relationship with God. He resented the times he found me in my favorite spot in the basement on my knees, praying behind the furnace. He would angrily say, "You are telling God on me now, aren't you?"

He felt guilty and tried to punish me for my relationship with God. When he found me listening to preaching on the radio, he angrily turned it off and cursed. Only praying and reading my Bible kept me sane enough so that my mind never snapped.

He kicked me from bed so often that I dreaded to go to bed before he came home. I began making a pallet on the floor between the girls' beds when he was out. I feared for my life because of his behavior. He needed help but refused counseling. After I endured 11 years of his abuse, God gave me a dream. It reminded me of how He warned Joseph by dream to flee to Egypt with Mary and baby Jesus, as their lives were in danger.

My dream was a night vision that began as I walked hand in hand with my husband, on a narrow bridge over the water. Suddenly, a violent storm arose; rain came in torrents, as lightning flashed and thunders rolled! I held his hand so tightly and said, "We must turn back to land." I looked back, and there was no land in sight and no place to escape. It appeared that we were in the middle of an ocean in great danger!

Suddenly, the scene changed, and I saw multitudes of people, as though it was earth's entire population. They were all in the water struggling for survival. No one else was on the bridge with my husband and me. The bridge was so narrow that only two could walk side by side. There was a handrail on the bridge, so I held to my husband with one hand while holding to the rail with the other. In my vision I was frightened and frozen with fear as the storm's fury rapidly intensified.

As the water rose rapidly higher, my visual scene changed. Suddenly, a loud voice from Heaven said, "Turn loose and follow me." I said, "Lord, I cannot turn loose because I cannot swim."

Then I held my husband's hand tighter as the angry storm raged on. I was aware the water was violently churning and now covered the bridge floor. The water continued rising rapidly as people in the stormy water were struggling to survive the storm.

The water on the bridge rose to my waist and was now to the top of the handrail. Then God's voice spoke out again as loud as thunder saying, "Turn loose and follow me." I answered Him again saying, "Lord, I cannot turn loose because I cannot swim."

Once more His voice was silent for a short time as the storm raged on. I was frightened and held tighter to my husband's hand as the raging waters rose to my chin. In my vision, I held my head as high as possible, to keep the water from covering my nose. I was keenly aware of struggling multitudes in the stormy waters and wondered if any of us would survive the storm.

Then God's voice spoke above the thunder's noise a third time saying, "Turn loose and follow me." Again I spoke back and said, "Lord, I cannot turn loose because I cannot swim."

Instantly, I thought that I would surely perish if I did not obey the voice of the Lord. My mind raced, thinking, "What have I got to lose? If I do not obey the Lord's command, then I will surely perish in the raging stormy water."

Quickly, I let go of my husband's hand. Instantly an object that looked like a round, rubber float fell from Heaven around my shoulders. I was quickly swept away by a strong force that separated me from my husband forever. I was transported to shore. I was not aware of the length of time that it had taken to sail through the vast multitude of struggling people. I landed safely on a white beach and was grateful I had not drowned in the storm. I stood up and the object that carried me to safety fell to the sand at my feet.

God had rescued me from the dangerous stormy water that otherwise would have been my grave. As I stood, I looked up and down the shore and was troubled to see that only a few had made it to shore by obeying the voice of the Lord. I looked back to the churning sea, and was grieved that no one in the water had survived. They had all perished in watery graves. I cried out to God because no one had rescued them from the raging storm!

I awoke from my vision scared, stunned, and crying. I ran to the basement to pray. I said, "Lord, what do you want me to do?" The answer He gave was, "Turn loose and follow me." My girls were small. I waited four years as God planned my departure.

Daily I prayed about my situation, and supernaturally things started to unfold. God answered my prayers. He gave me a job in town and gave me strength to go to work although I was not physically well. I began paying on a car and saving for a down payment on a new mobile home. For four years I saved, but God protected me as He unfolded the steps of His plan.

During those four years, the vision was strong on my mind. I had money deducted from my monthly piecework salary, so that my husband never suspected I was saving for a plan of escape. Although I was sickly, I worked faithfully to get the down payment for my home. Four years later a new life with my young daughters began. God supernaturally gave me a cosigner, to sign my banknote at the place where I purchased my mobile home.

It would not be easy as a sickly, 37-year-old, but I knew that I could trust God. He had led my life this far.

Now He was providing a way for us to escape my husband's abuse. I had no choice but to trust God for our daily survival.

Satan shattered my dreams, my home, and my marriage. I had desired a peaceful home and a loving husband. Now all I had were my daughters and the Lord. I leaned heavily upon Him to carry me through my bad times. Without God, I could not have made the big step to establish a home for my girls and myself at age 37, especially with my poor health.

One day while my husband was at work, we packed my car with our personal belongings. We hugged our dog and cat, kissed them good-by, and left. It was sad leaving our beautiful shepherd dog and our cat, but they could not go along. Animals were not allowed in the city location where we were headed.

In June of 1965, as we left for Winston-Salem, North Carolina, I felt as though I had pulled up my roots. Although my heart ached for the home I had grown to love, I never again returned to our home to live. God helped me cut the ties.

Since I had become so frail, I knew that surely I must live by faith in the God I had served and had trusted with my life since childhood! God was leading my way as I drove off that day. Tears filled my eyes but I never looked back!

God had made a way for us to escape the danger we lived in for so long. Although I was relieved to be free, it was painful to pull up roots and follow God's plan for my life. I felt just as Abraham must have felt, not knowing what my future held, but my trust remained fully in God!

Chapter 4

A New Life

In June 1965, the three of us began a new life. My girls were ages 10 and 13; I was 37. Through domestic court, their daddy paid $12.50 weekly, per child. That amount never paid even half of their doctor bills, food, clothes, or school expenses.

There were times their daddy missed a week's payment, and times I scarcely knew where our next meal would come from, but God always provided. I never had to ask anyone for help. After I paid tithes, God met our financial needs just on time. Those were hard years, yet the many hours I prayed paid off.

My girls and I attended every service at a denominational church. At church, often after I shook hands with someone, I would find a twenty-dollar bill left in my hand. That money helped supply food for the day. I graciously thanked God for filling our need.

I never missed one payment on our new home, nor did I miss one payment on other bills. They were paid on time and we had food to eat. We thanked God for pretty clothes. I had been experienced as a seamstress, so we were always nicely clothed. Although my pay was small then, I knew how to budget. My pastor's wife said that I was a great money manager, and she complimented us on dressing so well despite my small salary.

Our weekdays passed quickly when I was working and my girls were at school. But the weekends dragged, especially during the winters. On Sunday afternoons, the girls and I would cry. It was too cold to go out to our park activity. We had time to reminisce, and we were missing our home, our shepherd dog and our cat.

Divorce is a touch of hell. We were crushed, yet we were relieved to be out of an abusive situation. I had planned to be married for life and never thought of getting divorced. I took our wedding vows seriously and had been determined to stick it out. God removed me from the abuse and salvaged my life.

Frustration and deep hurt filled my heart, as the one I had trusted in marriage turned out to be so abusive. I had no one to counsel with, so it took ten years for my broken heart to heal before I could trust again. Throughout all of my trials I stayed close to God and He carried me through my tough times.

I needed a Christian counselor, but I did not know one. So I can sympathize with those having their homes destroyed by divorce. It is extremely vital to get over hurts and pain from the abuse quickly, so disease cannot destroy the physical body.

Grief is a vicious killer and I certainly had my share of it. That was before I learned how to loose the evil spirits and cast my cares on Jesus. It took a lifetime to learn to let Jesus bear my load so that I could gain victory!

The Holy Spirit is my Great Comforter and Teacher. If I had been baptized with the Holy Spirit back then, I could have overcome my trials with much less pressure. Although I was saved very young, I was not taught the Spirit baptism. But thank God, in 1986, while on my first tour of Israel, I received the wonderful Holy Spirit baptism that impacted my life.

What a difference God's Spirit baptism has made for me! The experience fine-tuned my spirit, filling me with peace and joy within. Upon receiving the baptism, I felt His presence so strongly that for more than three weeks my flesh kept tingling.

When we miss the Holy Spirit baptism experience, we miss one of the greatest experiences in life. This baptism prepares us for God's service. However, at that time I was unaware that God was preparing me for His service. His Spirit changed my temperament from timidity to boldness. Now instead of being shy in crowds, I am bold enough to teach them.

However, it was many years before my broken heart healed. It took ten years for me to get over the shock of my divorce. I poured my life into my job, my girls, and my church activities. I had no time to waste and no desire to date. I was hungry to get closer to God and overcome the many satanic attacks.

In all my attacks, I was not aware that Jesus had defeated satan and won my battle. I did not know that Jesus had delegated to me power to overcome my enemy, and power to keep demonic activity under my feet. (See Luke 10:19.) I only knew I must live above sin or be destroyed by satan, and that my life and frail body depended entirely upon my relationship with God.

My health was rapidly declining from the unhappiness of having been married to an abusive husband for 15 years. By then I had experienced 12 surgeries and had been hospitalized 20 times. Leaving my girls and going to the hospital so often grieved me because I knew I was their security and protection. I tried to make up for a lack of devotion that their dad showed them.

I dedicated my life to care for them. I spent as much time as possible taking them on picnics in the park on Sunday afternoons. I am aware they missed a lot growing up by not having the companionship of a father. But the tradeoff was that we had peace and relief by not being in an abusive situation.

Before we had separated my girls would say, "Mother, please take us away from Daddy's abuse," yet after our divorce they still loved and missed him. He seldom cared to take them home for a weekend visit, and when he did he talked against me. I never tried to turn them against him. Instead, I left the justice to God. I was not filled with hate, but I was filled with pain, hurt, and a broken heart, until God healed my wounds.

Later, one daughter had no money to buy her dad a Christmas present. She was reluctant to visit her dad that Christmas. I gave her a small gift to give him and encouraged her to visit him. She said that during the visit he constantly put me down, and that grieved her. I had taught forgiveness no matter how badly one is treated. My divorce was hard on my girls, but our trials taught them a lot, and I'm so proud of them!

For 13 years after the divorce my daughters and I lived together before they married. I loved and nurtured them the best I physically could. I hated leaving them alone when I was in the hospital while they were teenagers. Satan kept his attacks coming. I never knew when Jesus would call me to Heaven, so I stayed close to God. He kept me alive through many attacks, and I learned to depend upon Him.

Before I learned that satan was the villain destroying me, I had experienced many surgeries. I relate many of my experiences hoping to save you from similar pitfalls, or to point a way out if you are now in an attack! You must keep your joy no matter how severe the attack, so the attack will end more quickly.

On August 7, 1970, I had major surgery. At that time, my older daughter had graduated from high school and had been working for one year. My younger daughter had two more years before graduation. I had stood by them through thick and thin, so my emergency surgery was a time of great distress for them. They faced the possibility of losing the security of their mother.

Satan is cruel. His mission is to "steal, and to kill, and to destroy" (John 10:10a). I was not aware that Jesus had come to give me a more abundant life. Oh, how I wish I had known, back then, that God's Word could have spared me from many sorrows!

I did know that I had two choices. One was to take the road of least resistance, which was the deception of satan's death trap. The other road was to resist him, to fight and refuse to give up. I chose to stay close to God and fight for my life. Our local church never taught me that I could gain victory over the deception of sickness, or that I could stand against my enemy by using God's Word. I was at war with an enemy and didn't know how to win. I want you to know that I beat all the attacks that came against me, and you can beat them as well!

Previously, I mentioned the migraine headaches that I endured in the late 1950s and 1960s. Finally, the reason for the migraine headaches was discovered in August 1970. One day when I was at work, a filling from a tooth in my upper jaw fell out. My jawbone ached badly, so I went to a dentist for x-rays. He found no abscess, but stated that my tooth needed to come out. It was now only a hollow shell without a filling.

The dentist gave me a shot to numb the jaw area, then proceeded to pull my tooth. I felt my jawbone breaking and pulled at his arm trying to stop the procedure. But he continued tugging at my tooth. When the tooth came out, there was a portion of my jawbone attached to each side of the tooth!

The dentist realized that he had created a hole that led into my sinus cavity, but he just stitched the skin over the area of the hole. He then packed my mouth with cotton gauze and sent me home without any antibiotics to prevent infection.

My jaw area bled profusely that night. I called my dentist's home twice, asking for help. He simply told me to put a Lipton teabag in my mouth and leave it there for 20 minutes; then to remove it for 20 minutes; and to repeat the procedure using a fresh teabag. Although I followed instructions, my bleeding continued.

By morning I was very weak, yet I drove to his office so he could repack the area. I was not given antibiotics that day for infection either, and I left his office in great pain. I missed only one day on my job even though I didn't feel like working. I had to pay a mountain of medical and hospital bills, along with my last dentist bill, so I went to work.

One week after my tooth extraction, I lost the hearing in my ear on the side where the tooth came out. Thank God it was a temporary hearing loss! In desperation I called a doctor's home that night to inform him of my condition. His name was Dr. William Allsup, Sr., and he had the reputation of being the best surgeon in the Winston-Salem area. He said that my hearing loss could definitely be related to the recent tooth extraction.

Because of the seriousness of my condition, he told me to come to his office the next day at 8 a.m., waiving the three-month waiting period. He was concerned that an infection might spread quickly to my brain. Because I had never been a patient of his before, his concern showed genuine dedication.

The next day I was Dr. Allsup's first patient. After examination, he sent me for x-rays. Unfortunately, infection had already spread dangerously throughout the sinuses. It was so serious that it would have to be controlled before he could perform the emergency surgery I needed.

I was given large doses of Mycin antibiotic four times daily. He instructed me to call if I needed help, and assured me that he would come to my rescue even if he had other patients scheduled. He went as far as to tell me to call him in the middle of the night if I needed his help.

His statement stunned me. I had never had a doctor say that before. I felt blessed to have a doctor who truly cared. Because I was momentarily speechless Dr. Allsup firmly said, "Do you understand how serious your condition is? And will you promise to call me if you get in serious trouble?" I said that I would, but I realize now that I did not understand how serious my condition really was. I just took one day at a time and went each day to his office for checkups. I wondered when I would be ready for the surgery that I dreaded so badly.

During my first visit, Dr. Allsup informed me that the surgery I needed was as serious as open-heart surgery. He said that the surgery involved operating close to my brain. I decided then that I did not want that surgery. Instead, I wanted to trust God for healing. I realize now that I lacked faith and was only hoping for healing. Ignorance is just hoping for healing, without having true healing faith based on the Bible.

Dr. Allsup continued checking me daily, then after one week he said that flesh was growing across my naked jawbone. It was trying to heal. Quickly I said, "Dr. Allsup, please do not operate; I know that I will be all right." So, because I persuaded him, he gave me a while longer before surgery.

My doctor had cautioned me on my first visit not to get wet in the rain. So for three months I avoided getting caught in a rain shower while I was on the Mycin antibiotic. It appeared that all danger was past until I got soaked in a thunderstorm one day. I drove my car 50 miles home in wet clothing. By the time I arrived home I was so tired that I never gave one thought to my doctor's warning that I was not to get wet in the rain.

That Sunday was a long hot day, and satan had beaten me down so much that my ability to fight for survival was just about gone. I did not realize that he was the author of all those physical attacks. I thought I just had bad luck. By bedtime I was tired and my body ached as though I had the flu. After stripping my wet clothing, I bathed and went to bed exhausted.

The next day I had my regular examination at Dr. Allsup's office. I was not feeling well and I told him that I was aching all over. He punctured through to my sinus cavity above the area where the tooth had been extracted. Then he began flushing the area with water. Only clear water came out, so he thought I was doing well. He said that my nerves might be frazzled because I had worked all those three months while taking strong antibiotics.

On the last day Dr. Allsup examined me, no infection showed up, so again he thought I was doing well. Without complaining I continued working, whereas most people never would have! I am sure that fact swayed him to believe that I was doing well.

So that day, I left his office and went back to work. When I drove home from work that evening, I suddenly felt tremendous pressure in my jaw. It was in the same area where my tooth had been extracted. Upon arriving home, I placed a small mirror in my mouth so I could take a look at the area.

The place in my mouth where the dentist had created a hole through to my sinus cavity had burst open! A purplish-colored pouch extended down through the area where my tooth used to be. I was too exhausted to consider the seriousness of my condition.

I did not call Dr. Allsup that night. Instead, I bathed and rinsed my mouth out with peroxide, unaware of any eminent danger, and went to bed. Miraculously, I slept through the night totally unaware that I was in big trouble. Surely both God and my angels were watching over me that night. I was totally unaware that I would land in the hospital the next day. Although I was in grave danger of losing my life, I was not afraid. My life belonged to God and my trust remained in Him! Through it all He has never failed me!

Chapter 5

Serious Surgery, Remarriage, and Lupus Danger

Upon arising from bed the next morning, I again washed my mouth with peroxide. I did not feel well, but my bills had to be paid so I went to work at 7 a.m. I was at work 15 minutes when the purple-looking pouch in my mouth ruptured. The contents began oozing out, and I began to feel extremely ill.

I rushed to the company nurse, and she notified my doctor's office. He was operating that day so his receptionist instructed me to go home and go to bed. She said he would call when he had completed surgery. I drove home to lie down and wait for his call. His call came at noon, though waiting seemed as eternity.

On the phone I told Dr. Allsup my condition. He was stunned and asked if I could drive to his office. I said that I could be there in 20 minutes. He replied that he would meet me there. Though I was very ill I drove to his office to learn my fate.

In his office Dr. Allsup pumped water through my sinus and was shocked at what he saw. I bent over a basin and as I opened my mouth, contents of a ruptured tumor washed into the pan through an opening in the roof of my mouth where the dentist had made a hole into my sinus cavity. By accident, the dentist had created a hole through which the tumor could rupture. In God's plan, though, this was no accident, but a way for me to escape death!

For years that tumor abscess had been behind my brain in the back of my sagittal sinus area, encased in a pouch. It had caused the bones to decay throughout my sinus cavity and evidently had caused all those migraines in past years.

While I was in Dr. Allsup's office, about a cup of abscess washed out from the opening in my mouth! He was shocked and said that the abscess was located where it never would have been found if it weren't for the open hole the dentist created in my mouth. It may have ruptured later on my brain. Considering the end results, my dentist actually did me a favor!

When the doctor saw the infection, he quickly told his secretary to call the hospital. He informed her to tell them he had a critically ill lady and must have the operating room immediately, as this was an emergency. I said, "But, doctor, you told me three months ago that I was too serious for surgery. Now I have a temperature of 101 and I'm aching all over." He replied, "It is operate now or never because your condition is very critical. You must have surgery at once."

A Most Serious Surgery

On August 7, 1970, I was rushed into surgery for removal of a ruptured tumor at the back of my sagittal sinus, adjacent to my brain. My two daughters stayed at the hospital throughout surgery. Just before the anesthesiologist put me to sleep, Dr. Allsup bent over the operating table and asked if I had anything to say. I replied, "I'm ready." As I drifted off I whispered, "Jesus, hold my hand." I thought I was going to Heaven to be with Him. I had absolutely no fear as I faced possible death. However, I dreaded to leave my daughters, as I was all they had.

Before surgery we kissed and I asked them to meet me in Heaven if I did not survive surgery. Hours later, my daughters surprised me, saying, "Wake up, Mother, open your eyes and see if you have vision in your right eye." I was shocked and thought, "Oh no, this is not Heaven. I do not want to endure more pain." They kept insisting, "Wake up, Mother." As I awakened, reality quickly set in and I realized I was not in Heaven. Then I realized that my pain was not over yet.

I could see with my eye and also feel all the pain from surgery. I endured pain without pain medication as Dr. Allsup said the infection was so close to my brain. He said mental alertness was vital in determining my condition. I looked into a mirror and was shocked. The right side of my face was swollen twice the size of my left side. I really looked pathetic indeed.

Soon Dr. Allsup came in and gave orders that I was not to lie in one position for more than 20 minutes at a time. He said I was to drink liquids as much as possible by using a straw, both day and night. The liquids would help wash away the residual poisons that had gone into my bloodstream during surgery. He said that God alone knew how serious my condition remained. He said that I still had only a 50 percent chance of survival.

Dr. Allsup placed me on maximum dosage of the same antibiotic I had taken for the past three months. He said the bones in my right sinuses had all decayed to the very edge of my brain. He also said he had removed two more cups of abscess in the operating room.

He then informed me that I must fight for my life if I wanted to live. He stated that I was like one straddling a fence, and that only God knew which way I may go. He urged me to be brave, as he could not prescribe any pain medication. He said that my mental awareness must be checked every 20 minutes to make sure no residual infection reached my brain.

A Painful Recovery

I had a painful recovery time, but was grateful that Dr. Allsup had saved my life. I told him that if ever my surgery needed repeating, I would choose death over the pain from that procedure. He was, though, a great, caring, compassionate doctor indeed!

On the fifth day after surgery, Dr. Allsup examined my mouth to observe the place where he had done plastic surgery to close the hole the dentist had made. Upon examination he said he could see that I had never smoked cigarettes or drunk alcohol. I was shocked and asked, "How can you tell that by looking in my mouth?" He said, "People who smoke or drink don't heal as quickly as you are healing."

When satan's big attack came, he could not utterly destroy me as I was walking close to God. Again, his destructive plan to take my life was defeated by my dedicated doctor. I would have died without his skilled surgery. God used Dr. William Allsup, Sr. to save my life so I could get well and enjoy many more years of life. My health improved, I was dismissed, and I never saw Dr. Allsup again for 20 years. After surgery I worked two jobs to pay my hospital and medical bills.

I Met and Married Jesse Dotson

By mid-1974 I was alone as my daughters were gone from home. Then I met Jesse Dotson. We were the same age and had much in common. He was reared in the country only 15 miles from where I grew up. He knew my mother's people. At times he had gone to my grandfather's stone-ground roller mill to purchase flour. Yet, we had never met until then, when we were in our mid-forties.

I remembered how badly my ex-husband had abused me, so I was not interested in dating. I was cautious and never dated for ten years. But I never enjoyed being alone. Jesse was my first male friend. I only wanted a friend to talk to by phone, but I got a surprise during that first phone conversation. I was surprised to find that each of us had only two children, and they were both daughters with identical names. What a shock! We each had one daughter named Wanda and one daughter named Donna. I never knew a coincidence as that. So I consented to have dinner with Jesse.

We went out to dinner off and on for five years before getting serious. Our friendship grew into love and then we were married in April 1979. Four months after our wedding I received a lupus diagnosis, which caused great stress upon our marriage.

Reunited With Dr. Allsup

In 1990 Dr. Allsup heard I was still alive. He re-·quested I meet with him at a nursing home where his aunt lived. It was great to see the one who had saved my life 20 years prior. He took me in his arms, giving me a bear hug. He was delighted that I was looking so well. I introduced him to Jesse, then he asked me to fill in the gap of the 20 years. So I informed him in detail of all that had happened for those past years, with the following:

I said, "Dr. Allsup, after you operated on me and saved my life, I had several illnesses, plus a back injury. Nine years after you did my serious surgery I received my lupus diagnosis."

Then I relayed how Jesse and I were married in 1979 while I was working for AT & T. I told him that after we married, I had an accident and fell on cement when leaving work. My fall injured my back. After two months and my back did not heal, my company doctor at work took blood samples checking for the reason.

Meanwhile, I was to take a daily 20-minute moist heat treatment at the nurse station. One day as I finished my treatment and proceeded to my work station, my company doctor said she had my test results. She said my news was bad, as the report showed I had an incurable collagen disease. Her statement utterly stunned me! I wondered what my outcome would be.

Slowly, I made my way back to my station to continue working. I tried to choke back my tears. I was grateful that it was time to go home. My co-workers were scurrying about, happy to be leaving for the day. But I was still stunned from my bad medical report. All hope for my future had just been stripped away, and I felt cold and numb inside.

I could not share my bad news with my co-workers. Neither could I hold back my hot tears. They began streaming down my face as the bell rang to go home. Now I could leave and no one would see me cry. As I drove home, my tears kept flowing and I wondered how I could tell Jesse my bad news. We had only been married four months. I waited until late that night, then I told him of my diagnosis. I assured him that my doctor was wrong. I told him that no way was I going to die! I kept my promise, though in 1980, I was told that I had been 24 hours from death.

Our greatest marriage test was the stress from lupus. We endured more than three years of testing while I was so ill. I struggled to hold my job at AT & T as lupus had caused liver failure. Nightly after work I made trips to Dr. Fred Klenner in Reidsville, North Carolina. He saved my life in 1980, when I had liver failure. Daily I would lie in his office while he pumped megadoses of vitamins into me intravenously. That way I could live, have insurance, hold a job, and pay my medical bills.

My body looked like a pincushion from the needles and shots. Miraculously my liver started functioning again. But lupus remained until I gained knowledge of how to stand on God's Word and act upon His Word by faith until my healing manifested.

As I mentioned earlier, the stress from lupus took its toll on our marriage. In June 1982, Jesse and I separated. The twelve months following our separation were horrible. It felt so terrible to be dying alone from lupus complications. I wanted to hide away, and once again I had no one to help me but God.

Then in January 1983, I was prayed for and told to speak God's Word over my condition. I obeyed and 12 months later my healing manifestation came. After my healing, Jesse and I were reunited in December 1985 when his house burned down.

When I had filled Dr. Allsup in on the past 20 years, he asked to look inside my mouth to observe how the plastic surgery, which he had done 20 years prior, had held up. He was so delighted to see that my scar had almost vanished away.

He said that many with lupus go into remission at some point, but then they may have another flare up. He was delighted that I was pronounced healed for many years, by Dr. Metcalf, my rheumatologist. Dr. Allsup said I was the first lupus patient that he knew of who was declared healed by a physician.

I told Dr. Allsup how I had changed my diet and how I daily took herbs, vitamins, minerals, and digestive enzymes. Furthermore, I had changed our diet by eliminating white sugar, food preservatives, and junk food. My appearance proved that my efforts had paid off. Then Dr. Allsup turned to Jesse, stating, "Well, Jesse, you must be the healthiest you have been in a long time."

Dr. Allsup insisted that I visit his son who had taken over his practice, as he had retired two years prior. He said he had told his son about me and that his son would be delighted to meet me. Then I hugged Dr. Allsup as Jesse and I told him goodbye. No words can describe my appreciation for his kindness!

The other doctor who saved my life was Dr. Fred Klenner. He has gone on to Heaven to get his reward for his kindness and true dedication! He was a wonderful doctor.

Dr. William Allsup will also get his reward in his appointed time. Without these two doctors, I would have died. With God's faithfulness and the doctors' help, I overcame that demonic attack!

Satan tried to divide my home and destroy my marriage. But I trusted God by using His Word and won that battle as well. Our spouse may not understand the battle, as satan attacks, as he tries to stop God's calling upon our life. But prayer changes things and it can accomplish more than counseling can. Everyone must learn patience and prayerfully give their spouse over to God!

By striving to stay close to God, Jesse and I have endured the storms of illness that satan sent. My body endured also! Satan is the author of misery, sickness, and divorce. He hates God's children, especially families. Remember, unless God is the center of a home, that home cannot survive satan's evil attacks.

With Jesus in our marriage we have survived 21 years since we learned who our enemy is. We learned how he operates. "With God all things are possible" (Matt. 19:26b). Thank God that time heals the hurts of broken hearts. So never despair, turn your hurts over to the Master and look to Him for the cure!

I have always forgiven quickly; however, I allowed hurts, sorrows, and grief to steal my joy and peace. That is how I fell into satan's trap. Since then, I have learned how to resist my cares and lay them on Jesus. This way I can keep my joy and win my faith battle no matter what comes my way. When pressures mount up I just take a deep breath, and say, "Jesus will help me through this trial." Then I leave the pressure there with Him.

The act of loving and forgetting all the hurt and pain from the past or even the pain of the present will keep us from falling into satan's deception trap. It surely is easier to stay out of his trap than it is to do battle and climb out later.

So keep your joy, and forget the pain of the past no matter how bad it may have been! Let Jesus carry your load. Take a lesson from me; forget all the bad things so that you can keep your joy! Then you can leave the defeat mentality behind you and go on in victory. If you will only obey my advice you can stay joyful and keep on serving Jesus! Amen!

Chapter 6

Details of My Healing
From Lupus

One night in January 1980, my kidneys failed. I was ravaged by pain and fever for 23 hours. My temperature ran 101-102 degrees all night and I felt I would not live until daylight.

I was weak and in excruciating pain as morning finally arrived. I could scarcely telephone my rheumatologist. When I was able to call, there was no answer. My entire body was wracked in pain as kidney poison went throughout my body. I knew I must get help quickly or I would not live, so I made another call.

I called another doctor whom I knew well. He advised me to rush to the emergency room. I said, "I cannot go to a doctor who is unfamiliar with my medical history." I thought that if this was my time to go, then I chose to die at home. I was not afraid, so I hung up the phone; I was so tired of suffering.

I stood for one moment, then I took one step toward a lounge chair; I felt I would pass out. Suddenly God spoke abruptly and clearly, saying, "You do not need to die; obey Matthew 18:19." I was stunned! His statement came as a total surprise. I never imagined that God would speak so clearly and distinctly. I had suffered all night without one word from God.

Quickly, I called a friend and related God's message. I hung up the phone and made my way to a chair and, as I recall, I passed out. When I regained consciousness two hours later, my kidneys were totally healed. My temperature was normal; my pain was gone. God healed my kidneys as I trusted and placed my life in His hands. My kidneys were healed, but the lupus remained!

Lupus took its toll on my body and my marriage. Although my kidneys were healed, other lupus symptoms began. As I stated before, stress caused Jesse and me to separate for three years. As I lay alone in bed I felt there was no medical help. I was allergic to most antibiotics. I was very ill and had almost lost all hope. Then one day a lady visited me, as I lay there so ill. She called a Rev. Smith and his wife to come visit me. That day in 1983 my hope for healing from lupus began.

On January 21, 1983, Rev. Smith opened his Bible to First Peter 2:24 and told me, "By the stripes of Jesus we were healed. 'Were' means already done!" I said, "I don't feel healed!" He said, "Satan gives lying symptoms." I told him that my doctor had said that I was in the final stage of lupus with no known cure. He had said that each remission would get shorter. He said that from then on, I would be in the hospital more than I would be home.

Rev. Smith then asked, "Who are you going to believe, a doctor's report or God's Word?" I told him that I would rather believe God as I did not want to die. He said, "All right, the choice is yours." He then cursed lupus and commanded my body to line up with God's Word, saying that I was healed as he ended his prayer. I stated, "I do not feel healed." He told me that feelings had nothing to do with changing the fact of God's Word. He said satan gave lying symptoms and if I believed a doctor's report, I would die; if I believed God's report I could live.

In my mind I had many questions. So I asked, "Do you really mean that I have a choice in this life and death battle?" He replied, "Yes, you do have a choice—to live, or to die." Then hope came into me because of the good news that I could choose my fate. I quickly chose life because I wanted to live.

I was 5 feet, 4-1/2 inches, with a medium frame, but my weight had dropped from 125 to 97 pounds. I was very ill, yet my attention had been aroused that day because it was the first time I heard God's wonderful report. By faith, I trusted God's Word, which said I was healed. Though I was a sick skeleton too weak to walk, I made a choice to believe God's report.

That day, as Rev. Smith laid hands on me, I felt no anointing. I chose to believe the Word. I took Mark 16:18b to be true. Paraphrased, "Believers shall lay hands on the sick, and they shall recover." Truth is simple; we must not complicate it! First, believe it; secondly, obey it; thirdly, receive it!

That day I believed; I obeyed, and made a documentation that read as follows: "Today on January 21, 1983, at 1:45 p.m., I am receiving my healing by faith in the report of Isaiah 53:5 and First Peter 2:24." I believed God's Word despite my long road to recovery. I had miserable, sleepless nights with pain before victory came. Satan's bad thoughts flooded my mind, but I never believed his suggestions or allowed the pain to stop my faith.

Before my healing manifested, my doctors had treated me with three drugs that are extremely harmful if used for an extended length of time. The doctor told me that one of the drugs could cause eye damage and possibly even blindness. At one point, I almost lost my vision.

Then one night at a cottage prayer meeting, I requested prayer for my eyes. The next morning, my eyes were totally healed and I read my Bible all day! Though my eyes were healed, lupus symptoms remained. Those symptoms received less attention from me. I was too busy thanking God for healing my eyes and acknowledging Him as my Healer and my Miracle Worker.

Three months after I was first prayed for, I went to Dr. Norvel Hayes's church in Cleveland, Tennessee. While there, I bought a tape set that taught me how to stand on God's Word to keep my healing. His tapes gave me courage to stand in faith, without wavering, until my victory came. Back then his tape set was my only source of teaching other than my Bible.

For one year, I trusted and confessed God's Word for my lupus healing. I learned that pain and symptoms are satan's way of deceiving and sidetracking us, trying to make us forget God's report. God's report was hard for my mind to grasp back then. But I was willing to reach for my last ray of hope.

God's Word worked, but not until my diet changed and I believed and faithfully confessed His Word. For 12 months, I fed both my spirit and my body. Only then did my faith grow stronger. Our physical body cannot be healthier than our diet; neither can our spirit prosper more than our diet of God's Word.

With my church's support, and Dr. Hayes' tapes, strength came for me to confess healing. My spirit never wavered though satan gave me bad thoughts. I rejected negative thoughts, bound up his suggestions, and cast them out. (See Matthew 18:18.)

Satan said I was stupid as I told people that I was healed. My pain seemed to contradict my words. I could not gain a pound, I continued experiencing pain. Satan left as he saw he could not make my faith waver. So did his symptoms. That proved that pain is a deceptive, lying spirit. Pain cannot alter God's Word unless I believe my pain overrides God's Word. To believe that lie shows an incomplete understanding of God's Word.

My doctor continued checking my blood semiannually for almost seven years and never found a trace of lupus. He found it hard to believe that I was the same person who had suffered so much. At times it is hard for me to believe that I am that person. My doctor now knows there are miracles. He said, "Healing of lupus is not in a doctor's vocabulary. Yet it appears that you are one that's healed!" He released me from his care, knowing for certain that God had healed me of lupus!

Thank God I am healed; I give Him all glory and praise! He was faithful to His Word. Jeremiah says God hastens His Word to perform it (see Jer. 1:12b KJV). God confirmed His Words as my body was healed. Two years after my healing God restored my marriage at the time when Jesse's house burned up.

Our victory comes from God's Word. "For the law of the Spirit of life in Christ Jesus has made me free from the law of sin and death" (Rom. 8:2). As we study God's Word, we can find hope therein. When we feed our mind on God's Word, that Word can give life, and change defeat to victory! (See John 1:1,4.)

I could not gain one pound until I stood on God's Word. As satan saw that I would not waver, he left and took my symptoms with him. That year, I put my weight back on and reached my normal 125 pounds. Since then, my weight has remained stable. Lupus vanished as my life of victory came from trusting God.

In January 1991, though, satan again attacked me with a back injury. It was my second back injury as my spine was weakened by the large amounts of drugs I had been given years before. My orthopedic surgeon said that surgery was not possible in my case and that I would always be an invalid. Once again, I never lost my hope or my faith that God would heal my body!

As I lay paralyzed for three months, unable to move a hand or a foot, I faithfully applied healing Scriptures to my back and then I was healed. By confessing the Word my doubts changed into unwavering faith in God's ability. Once again, a doctor's report of defeat turned my defeat report into victory! I applied God's Word continually and God sent His Word to heal my spirit, soul and body. His Word healed me! (See Psalms 107:20.)

I am a walking miracle, doctors say, because I overcame lupus, kidney failure, liver failure, and being paralyzed in bed for three months. I also had 12 surgeries and 20 hospital stays, so I feel indebted to God to share my testimony with others. If sharing is my debt to pay for my healing and the wealth of knowledge I gained through my experiences, then I am so willing!

We are our brothers' keepers. We cannot sit on the truth. We must share with others or we will be defeated. We overcome satan by the Blood of the Lamb and by words of our testimony (see Rev. 12:11a). Confessing God's Word made me overcome as I obeyed Mark 11:23 and spoke to the mountainous oppositions.

So many need help, but few are willing to work. In Luke 10:2a, Jesus said, "The harvest truly is great, but the laborers are few." God doesn't honor lazy people who disrespect Him by not making an effort to confess His Word. Never expect God to keep blessing you with healing if you are too lazy to read His Word, believe it, and confess it over pain from lying symptoms!

Though Jesus paid the price for healing, I cannot be guilty of ignoring the stripes Isaiah 53:5 says He bore for me. By Jesus' stripes I'm healed, but my part is to read and quote God's Word. Healing is a gift, but actions must agree with His Word as we are tested to prove that faith in His Word holds strong.

If we are looking for an easy way to be healed, we may not find it unless God chooses to shower His mercy on us with a miracle. At times, He does heal that way as anointed ministers lay hands on us. But the best way to be healed is to find our healing in God's Word. Then most likely we will stay healed.

To work effectively in God's vineyard our healing must remain stable. Wounded, sick workers are not as capable as strong ones. It takes healthy, strong ones to labor on the battlefield. Let us mend those broken, bleeding ones and bind their wounds. Be a "Good Samaritan" and lend a helping hand to those satan has wounded in battle. For years I was sick and wounded with no help. Now I have compassion to help the wounded!

There are many wounded soldiers on life's battlefields. If they lie without help, the enemy can destroy them. Let us carry them to safety and pour the oil of God's Word into their wounds.

God desires abundant life for everyone! John 10:10b says that Jesus came to give us a more abundant life. The abundant life is ours for the taking when we become obedient to God's Spiritual laws.

By obeying John 15:7, as we stay abiding in Jesus and live in the boundary of His Word, we can ask and get answers. We truly can turn a defeated life to victory by executing God's Word!

Chapter 7

Never Be Fooled by Deception

Satan must deceive our mind before he can destroy our body. If we believe God's Word and proclaim it, satan cannot destroy our body. Deception is satan's main weapon of destruction.

Before any deadly disease can destroy or kill me, I would have to believe that the devil's power to kill is stronger than God's power to heal. I would have to believe that God was unwilling to keep His healing promise of restoration. Then, by discouragement or deception, I would have to surrender to satan's deadly power, without tapping into God's healing power.

We must know that God has the greater power and that He desires that we accept His healing plan. It insults

God when we don't believe His covenant promises. If we walk in unbelief we are at the very place that satan desires. Then he bombards our minds with more doubt to wear us down. (See Daniel 7:25.)

When we talk of satan's attacks we give him glory. Then he takes advantage of that publicity. Instead, let us magnify God's Word and give Him our praises. As we give God praise, He is able, faithful, and willing to fight our battles.

Results come as we give the battle over to God and believe Him for an answer. We can believe God and live, or we may doubt His Word and die. My believing is my faith at work, so I must use my faith as a servant and put my servant to work.

God's True Report

I want to repeat the report in Isaiah 53:5: "But He was wounded for our transgressions, He was bruised for our iniquities; the chastisement for our peace was upon Him, and by His stripes we are healed."

God performs surgery in our body, as we trust His Word. Our faith and trust gives Him permission to operate so the healing process can begin. But all doubt must be turned to unwavering faith before God can do the surgery that we need so badly.

Our Complete Atonement

God's healing covenant was completed on the cross when Jesus said, "It is finished!" (See John 19:30). We must believe His covenant and accept His atonement plan for sickness as well as for our sin. God gave us a free will, so He gave us the freedom to make choices. God never makes choices for us.

If we look to the cross, we live. If we look away in unbelief, we can die. God is not to blame for our failures. If we fail it's because we have not talked enough to our mountainous problems as Jesus instructed in Mark 11:23-24. We must forcefully talk to problems, and then rely on what Jesus did on the cross. If we look to the cross, we believe the report in Isaiah 53:5, "By His stripes we are healed." (Already healed!)

All of us may face a decision someday whether to believe our doctor's report or whether to believe God's report. That's when faith is put on trial! Then whose report will you believe? I chose to believe God's report rather than my doctor's report that lupus would destroy and kill my body. That's when lupus lost its power over my spirit and body. My faith broke satan's death grip from off my spirit and set me free from deception!

I trusted God's report that Jesus had paid my healing debt by stripes on His back, and that He would honor faith for healing just as He honored faith for salvation. He was both able and willing, so my faith turned my sickness to health. The power of His Word worked in my heart and my mind, as I spoke God's Word.

Without active faith, emotions cannot rest, nor can we trust that God's Word will work. But it takes patience to wait on our promises. And patience never hurries...neither does God. So never try to rush Him. As we trust in God's credibility, our emotions settle down, and then we can patiently rest in His Word.

Look and Live

Although on Calvary Jesus paid both for sin and for our healing, it can only take effect when we accept His report through faith. Victory comes when we rely upon God's finished work on Calvary. By God's plan, we look and we live! Looking is trusting God's atonement plan for both body and soul without doubting His credibility to perform His promises! Amen!

John 3:14-15 says that as Moses lifted up the serpent in the wilderness, even so must Jesus be lifted up. By speaking the Word we lift up Jesus, and all who believe His plan will live.

That serpent in the wilderness represented the cross where Jesus was lifted up so sin could be canceled. All who look at Calvary in belief can live. This may sound too simple but it is true. So, trust without doubting. Read John 3:14-17 and Isaiah 53:5. If we believe God's report we will not perish but gain eternal life.

Our faith and trust give Jesus permission to do surgery on the cells in our body so that our healing process begins. Isaiah 53:1a says, "Who has believed our report?" So few truly look and live by trusting God's Calvary plan. Will you be one to trust His report and look to God's promises and live?

I am thankful that I dared to trust Isaiah's report. I came back from near death. No doctor was able to erase my death sentence or give me life. Only faith in what Jesus did at Calvary rescued me and enabled my healing to manifest. If you will dare to trust Isaiah's report, then God will do the same for you.

Faith Anchors Our Souls for Rest

When I believed God's Word was a true report, I began to act on it and so I put my faith in motion. My mind completely changed and became set on God's promise. This gave rest in my soulish realm and stabilized my thoughts and emotions. The sorrow that came with my death sentence left and joy took over the place where my sorrow had been! Observe how Jesus spoke of rest to those following His plan: "Come to Me, all you who labor and are heavy laden, and I will give you rest. Take my yoke upon you and learn of Me, for I am gentle and lowly in heart, and you will find rest for your souls" (Matt. 11:28-29).

Patience Makes Us Wait for God's Promises

As turmoil leaves our minds, patience makes us willing to wait for the fulfillment of God's infallible promises. The last part of Hebrews 6:12 says that through faith and patience we inherit the promises. When I discarded my doubt in God's ability to rescue me, anxieties ceased and I rested in His promises. I never fretted about how long it would take for my recovery to be complete. Resting in God taught me His Word and His ways.

As I learned about God's wonderful, loving nature, I thanked Him each day. I waited patiently on Him as He carried out His promise to heal my weakened, frail body. I refused to doubt His ability or His willingness because I knew He could not lie! I would never hunger or thirst again as I ate and drank daily from God's Word. His Word brought nourishment that strengthened my frail body. It brought victory to me as I continually meditated upon His Word. (See Psalms 1:1-3.)

God's Intensive Care Unit

Although my faith allowed Jesus to do surgery on my soul and my body, intensive care was needed after I had major surgery. I allowed Jesus to complete my healing process by placing my faith in Him and giving Him total possession of my will. After He did Holy Ghost surgery, I had a 12-month recovery period in God's intensive care unit. It took that long to heal me completely because I had been so wounded and frail.

Jesus so gently nourished me back to health and strength as I ate portions of His Word daily, hour by hour. His Word was medicine for my frail body. I was so thankful to Jesus for taking stripes on His back and spikes in His feet and hands for me, so I spent much time in worship and praise.

I rested each day in His loving care and drank of His promises. Truly I needed that rest! I learned to have patience because He was so patient with me. Then new life began flowing back into my sickly, frail body and I began slowly moving about.

First I was on crutches and then I began walking surefooted without crutches. Finally, I was running and dancing before the Lord. Jesus filled me with life, joy, and strength. One year later my recovery period ended and my work for Jesus began.

Freely I Received, Freely I Must Give

Through the truth from God's Word I had won the battle over deception. Now it was time for me to pass on to others the truth that God can lovingly care for them. There are so many who are in need of this healing message. Jesus expects us to help the needy, not to be lazy or self-centered by ignoring the wounded, battle-scarred ones that satan has struck down.

I must give to others as I have received. Matthew 10:8 says, "Freely you have received, freely give." I must teach people to patiently trust God and to help those in need. I have great compassion for the sickly and know that I must give them God's Words of life. Where would *I* be if no one had helped me?

Possessing the Soulish Realm

Luke 21:19 says, "It is by patience that we possess our souls." Our intellect and emotions are kept stable with our patience. Are you in possession of your soul? What is your mind kept on? Our life and outcome both depend upon our thought life!

If our mind and thoughts are not stayed on God's promises enough to fill us with joy, peace, hope, and faith, then we will be overcome by the cares of life. To rest in faith is one way to possess our soulish realm and keep the enemy at bay.

Perfect Peace Is in God and His Word

The amount of God's Word that we hear and put to practice in our lives determines how much peace and success we gain. Mark tells us, "Take heed what you hear" (Mark 4:24a). It's vital to hear the Word and get God's Word registered in our hearts so we can change a lifetime of bad beliefs or wrong teachings. Quoting God's Word reprograms my mind to agree with God's Word.

My mind cannot dwell on symptoms. I emphasize that if I trust God, peace controls my mind. I then give God permission to mold and reshape me so that my soul will rest in the trust of His Word.

In Jesus I found a place of complete rest for my soul. His services were free for my taking. But His gift cost Jesus His life. His services cost me no money;

but, my cost was a decision of compassion and dedication to serve Him with joy and delight.

I have dedicated my life to serving Jesus. I never knew real joy until I gave Him my all. I no longer worry about what people say about me. God set me free from caring about the opinions of others. My concern is on what God knows and thinks about me.

Death, Satan's Mission; Life, Jesus' Mission

Look again at John 10:10. Here we see that satan's mission is to steal, and to kill, and to destroy. Jesus said His mission was to give life more abundantly. By believing the mission of Jesus, my life changed into one of more abundance.

Jesus did His part. First John 3:8 says, "...the Son of God was manifested, that He might destroy the works of the devil." Our words will determine our outcome. They help us to believe God. The Bible tells us that the devil "is a liar and the father of it" (John 8:44b). Who wants to believe a liar?

God's Love Is Genuine

God's love is genuine, and He will do us no harm. Someone who truly loves us cannot do us harm. Love is never self-centered or unkind. Read John 3:16 to see how God so loved us, and then read Isaiah 53:5 to see how Jesus died in our place to prove the depth of His love. Read your Bible and meditate on the words of those verses and you will draw strength from His Word.

Again I say that Isaiah 53:5 is a two-fold atonement. Very few take the last part of that verse and act upon it. God's atonement means our souls have been redeemed from sin and our bodies are counted redeemed from sickness and disease as well. If you believe His Word, you will confess it with your mouth.

Are you speaking words that bring life or words that bring defeat and death? We must watch our words and never speak satan's report or bad symptoms. I will only speak God's Word the remainder of my life. Abundant life will then come to me by mediating and stating God's Word faithfully on a daily basis.

The Justice of Almighty God

God's laws are just. He only required one price for sin and transgressions. The price He charged was the precious Blood of Jesus. He charged sin's debt to Him, and Jesus paid the full penalty! Why should we pay, too? God never charged two people for our sin debt. Jesus paid my debt; my believing sets me free.

Do you think that because you are sick you are paying your own sin penalty? This is total deception! It is a useless price you pay in vain! You are paying a debt that has already been paid. Either Jesus has paid the debt, or you are paying it. Two people cannot pay the same debt. The only way you are justified to stay sick is by not believing Calvary's redemption plan!

When Jesus died on the cross for our sins, He went one step further. He paid for our healing with the stripes on His back. Oh, the depth of that love! Truly, truly, God is love.

Let God's love set your mind free so you can be healed. Suffer no longer; your ransom has been paid. To trust God's report positions us to be healed in our soul, our spirit, and our body, through God's power and through trusting in God's ability.

God's Ability and His Willingness

I have stated portions of God's love. Now I want to tell of His ability and His willingness. In Matthew 28:18 Jesus said, "All authority has been given to Me in Heaven and on earth." Jesus has all authority, so what do we fear? I never fear that satan can destroy me as long as I trust God! Deception is satan's greatest weapon, and fear gives deception its power.

Isaiah 54:17a says, "No weapon formed against you shall prosper." So what is there to fear? I live by God's Word that supplies bread to my hungry soul. It feeds and sustains me. His Word is my sword of protection and faith is my shield. As long as I live in God's Word I am safe from the enemy of fear!

Jesus is our Good Shepherd and He cares for His own. He has never lost one of His sheep. Read Psalms

91 and Psalms 23. These passages assure us of our Shepherd's Divine protection. The Lord truly is our Shepherd and we shall not want if we stay close to Him!

Jesus Delegated Power to Us

We mentioned earlier that Jesus has been given all power and authority. Jesus is now seated in Heaven, acting as our High Priest before the Father. When He left earth He said He would not leave us comfortless, but would send the Holy Spirit to lead and guide us into all truth. (See John 14:18; 16:13.) He gave us power to overcome deception. The Holy Spirit gives us the power to overcome satan's attacks if we obey God's instructions.

In Luke 10:19, Jesus transferred and delegated power to us, His disciples, but we must obey! We aren't defenseless; He delegated power above and beyond all the power of our enemy. That covers cancer, lupus, AIDS, diabetes, or any other enemy!

Although Jesus has already battled and won the war with satan. He equipped us well for our personal battle with our mind! Jesus holds the keys of death and hell, not satan. (See Revelation 1:18.) We never directly combat satan. The battle is fought within our mind and soul realm. Though satan is defeated, he battles to steal our faith in God and His Word from our hearts and minds.

We have nothing to fear as Jesus has all power and He has delegated power to us. He gave us His Blood, His Word, and His Name to use on satan. God's power is far greater, and I rest in the fact that He has never lost one battle. My mind is peaceful knowing that His power is available for me. Now I can surrender my will to Him and rest, knowing He holds all things in control.

No Power Is Greater Than God's Power

God's power to heal is far greater than satan's power to destroy. But a spirit of fear opens a door for satan to come through. Our faith closes that door so fear cannot destroy us. Do you see why it is impossible to please God without faith? (See Hebrews 11:6.) Without faith, I leave an open door for satan to intrude with a fear trap of deception. If fear gets in my mind, then my emotions take on satan's destructive thoughts.

We must shut the door to fear and seal it shut with faith. Then Jesus can operate and heal the wounds that satan has inflicted. Jesus gave us permission to use His Name to drive satan out. The Name of Jesus carries God's power and authority. The Name of Jesus has Heaven backing it up. Oh, what power His Name carries!

God's Willingness to Heal

Consider God's willingness to help us. Third John 2 says, "Beloved; I wish that you may prosper in all things and be in health, just as your soul prospers." According to this, God desires that our souls will prosper. But we can only prosper as our minds are filled with God's Word. According to the Book of Romans, a renewed mind will change our mental picture images. (See Romans 12:2.) Our answers come from mental picture images and expectations that are formed from God's Word.

Our Responsibility

Deuteronomy says if we seek the Lord with all our heart and soul, we will find Him. (See Deuteronomy 4:29.) It's our duty to seek and find God and apply His Word to our frazzled emotions.

Psalms 66:18 says, "If I regard iniquity in my heart, the Lord will not hear me." Our healing cannot manifest if God does not hear our prayers because of our iniquity. Our channel to God must be clear, so that He can hear and answer prayer. By controlling the thoughts of our mind we will win the battle over deception.

We must not seek healing before we seek Jesus Who is our healer. Then we must worship Him. "The Father is seeking such to worship Him" (John 4:23). Worship is our daily duty!

Worship and love must be top priority. If you love Jesus you will worship Him as your healer. As you find Jesus in His Word, you find healing. Your healing comes from God and from His Word, just as His Word healed me. (See Psalms 107:20.)

When we find Jesus, all our need is filled. In Matthew 5:6 Jesus said, "Blessed are those who hunger and thirst for righteousness, for they shall be filled." If we get hungry enough to meditate on God's Word, our soul will prosper. God's Words are "life to those who find them" (Prov. 4:22a). God waits for us to seek Him, and then He rewards us when we do.

The Word of God is food for our soul and medicine for our body. Since the Word is our bread and our medicine, we must eat of it daily. If sickness attacks we need more of His Word for medicine. When I was sick I stuffed myself on a daily diet of God's healing Word. Thereby, I got abundant health and abundant life.

When our minds are under attack we can stay calm by reading Psalms 91, which gives courage to help us overcome our attack. We are spirit beings so spirits must be fed on God's Spiritual Word. Jesus said His Word is bread for our life. (See John 6:35.) Therefore, meditating on God's Word enriches our lives!

The Bible is the only book I know of that contains the life of God inside its pages. John 1:1-2 informs us that God and His Words are the same. When I searched the Word I found what God was like, and I found He was different from the way religion had portrayed Him. He is loving, kind, and compassionate to those who seek Him because love and compassion is God's nature.

God is not punishing us for our sins as Jesus took our punishment. But God wants our repentant hearts to be in total surrender. He will answer if we sincerely seek Him with a contrite spirit, through prayer and daily Bible reading.

The life of God is inside the pages of His Word. Then our life is renewed from the pages of His Word. His Word is truth that sets us free from the enemy's negative way of thinking.

You can look in the mirror of God's Word and have your hope restored. Then happiness will change mental picture images. You can leave behind a defeated life of pain, sickness, and sorrow, and press on to victory. The renewed life of peace and happiness is found in Jesus by using His Word as a daily guide. Then you can go from defeat to victory just as I did! Amen!

Chapter 8

My Unique Ministry Calling

When God called me into the ministry in 1989, at the age of 60, I felt that I was one of the least qualified. I was like Jonah—I wanted to run! I gave God every excuse that I could, just why I was not qualified. I told Him that He made a big mistake calling me, because I had no Bible college training.

I am not in the teaching ministry by "self choice." I never wanted to stand before the public. Instead, I wanted to hide in crowds. Although I loved people very much, I felt shy and insecure when I stood before large groups of people. How God has changed my temperament! Crowds no longer bother me when I minister. Instead, I stand in reverential fear before

God, as I want to be His faithful servant and please Him above all others.

I feel that it was unique how God placed His ministry calling upon my life. I am not aware of another that received his or her calling in the same manner that I was called. God is awesome because He sure knew how to get my attention.

My background was in denominational churches, which taught against women in the pulpit. My husband agreed with this teaching, and since I was a female, my ministry calling created a problem! I wanted to run and hide as Jonah did! But I never outran God. He knew precisely how to catch me!

In 1989, I returned to Dr. Norvel Hayes's meeting. That was my first return visit since purchasing his tape set five years prior. The tapes had helped me keep my lupus healing. On the first day God awakened me crying aloud, at 6 a.m., before the service began. As I awoke I was startled; I jumped from bed and ran into the bathroom, trying not to disturb my friends who were sharing the room. The Holy Spirit was weeping uncontrollably through me. I fell on my knees saying, "Lord, what are you telling me?"

His Spirit wept through me, showing me visions of sick, suffering masses of people. Some were on cots and others were in wheelchairs. I said, "Lord, why are you showing me all those sick people?" His reply was that He wanted me to help them, and His Spirit continued to weep compassionately through my voice.

I gave God all kinds of excuses such as, "I am a woman, I am too old, and I do not have a college degree. Lord, you know my husband doesn't believe in women ministers." I said, "In fact, no one in my town believes in women ministers, and Lord, I'm incapable of fulfilling this ministry calling."

Yet, early the next morning while I am still in bed asleep, at the same time, the shaking and weeping repeated. He said, "Will you be a willing vessel that I can use?" Again I replied that I was not capable of fulfilling that calling.

Again the following morning, my bed began shaking at 6 a.m. As I ran to the bathroom and fell on my knees, He showed me the gravely ill and at the same time wept through me. I said, "I got the message the first day." Then I pondered why my vision had been repeated three times and three days, three consecutive mornings.

I believe the Lord spoke three different times, just as He did to Peter, so I would not forget my calling. He said, "You can help them. Will you do it for Me?" It was as though He was pleading. My emotions were mixed. I was afraid to say yes, and afraid to say no after three mornings of shaking and weeping.

On the third day, again I told God that I lacked ministry training. But He wept through my voice saying,

"If you are willing, I will qualify you as a vessel without Bible college training." His Spirit shook all my excuses out. I yielded to His calling and instantly the shaking and weeping ceased.

With great fear and reluctance, I agreed to tell my testimony, but not do teaching. I got up from my knees trembling and thought, "What have I gotten into?" Yet on the other hand I felt joyful. I certainly had mixed emotions about my calling. I'm sure this is why His Spirit came daily those three mornings to make sure I would obey. I admit it took a lot of coaxing on God's part to get me to obey His serious calling.

From the beginning I knew that it would not be my ability, but it would be the Lord's ability operating through me! When I minister now the Spirit operates through me, and He does the miracles. I know miracles are not performed by my power, or by my ability, but they are preformed by the Holy Spirit's power!

Although there is persecution in following Jesus as a woman, it is worth every trial. Jesus goes with us through our valleys. He is always there, and He feels our pain when we are hurting. He is there helping us as a constant companion through the trials that we encounter. He gives us great peace so that all we have to do is whisper His Name, because we are never alone!

I have never regretted answering God's call to serve His people. But answering His call as a female has not been easy. Yet my joy and inner peace is great as I minister in the Spirit's anointing. I am not a professional speaker at all, but His Holy Spirit fills in for my lack of ministry training.

At times I'm amazed and feel as though I'm another person as His Words come through my voice. I know those Words are His, not mine! God's Spirit is the greater One living in me. He makes up for my lack of Bible college teaching; I solely depend on Him!

God truly gets the credit! I remind myself I am nobody and He is everything! It amazes me that He chose one like me without Bible college training, and then shared His Spirit and wisdom with me. I am deeply humbled that He wanted me to work for Him.

My life's schedule was shifted as God called me to the ministry. My husband, Jesse, did not accept God's calling so well. He did not understand why our lives were interrupted. By that time, he had forgotten how satan had intruded by almost taking my life with lupus complications. His thoughts were, since I was well, why not go with him on trips to the mountains, instead of ministering to people in homes or in churches.

But my commitment to the sick and to Jesus was deep! Jesus helped me in a time of great need when I was alone without my husband or anyone else. When I was alone near death, Jesus was there healing and meeting my need. I really was never alone!

My husband Jesse fought the baptism of the Holy Spirit after we reunited. He had never believed in the experience. He persecuted me by saying I was in a cult. But praise God, he now has the Holy Spirit baptism! After his experience, he asked, "Why does my church teach this experience is not real?" I replied, "That is a good question, but the answer is deception." The experience is as real as God and His Word! If they would openly study the Bible they would know this experience is for today.

Before Jesse experienced the Spirit baptism, satan gave him a vision that I was a witch. Later, he watched Dr. Hayes's video entitled, "Worship, Worship God." That video took his blinders off, and then he got on his knees as Dr. Norvel Hayes did, and worshiped God. The power of God flooded through him and removed his doubts. He never returned to a church that teaches a doctrine of man that strips God's Word and makes it powerless.

So Jesse began speaking another language as the Spirit gave him utterance. He said, "I never felt the power of God before. Why has no one told me that this experience is real?" I replied, "I tried for seven years to tell you but you would not believe me." However, the encounter he had with the Holy Spirit somewhat softened the fact that God had definitely called me, his wife, as a female, into the ministry!

Very slowly he began to accept the call God placed on my life. However, he has not been one hundred percent happy about it. There have been adjustments in our lifestyle as I now share my time with the public. We aren't as private as we used to be. There are calls coming almost daily from hurting, wounded, sick ones.

Sometimes sympathy overwhelms my senses as compassion tries to take over my reasoning. Then satan tries to take advantage of my sympathizing heart. I have had to learn to spend more time with God than I spend with people. But that was difficult for me to learn because of my compassion for the suffering people.

Jesse would prefer for me to stay home and not travel so much, but the call is too great. I must help the suffering ones. Yet I know that their real help is from God, by spending more intimate time with Him. All that God wants is for us to totally surrender our hearts to Him in worship. We were created to have fellowship with Him and to worship Him. Until we learn how to worship God we will miss the entire purpose for our existence!

We will be easily tempted by satan to worship money, clothes, jewelry, vacations, boats, homes, and a host of other things, without taking time to worship God. The things I listed are not bad unless they come before our worship time with God!

Material things only become bad if we allow them to come before God as idols. Matthew 6:33 says, "But seek first the kingdom of God and His righteousness, and all these things shall be added to you." So we must not get the cart in front of the horse by putting things before our worship time with God!

Our approach to God must be corrected. It is God first, our desires thereafter. In Deuteronomy 5:7 God said, "You shall have no other gods before Me." That means we are not to have false gods or idolize anything other than God. When we put God first in our lives, He rewards us with much greater blessings.

The correct way to approach God is to seek His fellowship before seeking His blessings. Relationship is a must before asking for His blessings. Otherwise we show God no love or respect! Never make God feel second place. The right way is to seek God first and show Him our deepest respect!

We gladly will share gifts with those who show us respect, as we know they're loyal and genuine. God also knows when our hearts are sincere and our love is genuine. If we are serious in worship, we will receive from God's Hand as that is His plan. Delighting ourselves in Him will result in His meeting our every need!

Again in 1990 God visited me. He approached me in the same motel in Gatlinburg, Tennessee, while I attended Dr. Hayes's meetings. I was awakened from a deep sleep with a tremendous shaking at 6 a.m., just as one year before. This was the morning after all services had ended; it was the day we would go home.

The Holy Spirit shook me so much that my bed shook again, just as before. The lady in bed beside me jumped to her feet, saying, "What is going on?" I could not say one word. The Holy Spirit had started weeping through my voice again, just as He did one year prior to this. I shook for almost two hours.

God began talking to me; His Spirit spoke to my spirit and said, "I want you to teach people how to receive their healing by using My Word." I said, "Lord, my husband barely let me share my testimony when I ministered. That's all he accepted with his background." But God never gave up on me.

He kept shaking and weeping through me and so gently said, "You partially obeyed, now I ask you to teach My Word." Then gently He coaxed me. As I resisted silently, I wondered about my ability for His assignment. As I resisted, suddenly I spoke loudly saying, "No way, Lord!" One roommate saw my dilemma and said, "I don't know what that 'no' you said was about, but it appears that you have no choice; I believe you must say yes!"

Then I surrendered by saying, "Lord, I will teach, but I have no training or capability." He replied, "If you yield fully to my instructions, I will teach and use you." Again He assured me that He would qualify me for service. He said all He needed was a willing vessel. I said, "Okay, Lord. I will surrender to teach just as I had surrendered to share my testimony."

Instantly the shaking stopped. Slowly I moved to the foot of my bed where one roommate stood. Placing my hand on her head I said, "God wants to use you too." As I spoke that word, the Holy Spirit thrust me backward and I landed with a thud on my bed.

I have never heard such hilarious laughter come from anyone as came through my voice as I landed on my bed and began to roll. The Spirit was using my voice! I was conscious of His Spirit laughing hilariously through me; I was not doing it. His Spirit surely was happy as I surrendered to teach His Word!

The weeping and laughter Spirits both lasted a total of two and a half hours. I was not in control. Instead, the wonderful Holy Spirit was in control of both my spirit and my voice.

I was as one living in two worlds at one time. As God used my voice with laughter I heard one roommate say to the other, "I've never dressed a Spirit-drunk lady, but we must dress her and carry her to the car." I am a modest person, so instantly I thought, *Lord, let up with your laughter so I can get dressed!*

I could not say a word during my laughter encounter, yet God answered my request based on my thoughts. Instantly, His laughter Spirit ceased, and so did my rolling. I became sober and calm.

God surely has a sense of humor! If He could speak through a donkey, He could cry and laugh through me. I say this for those who doubt my genuine encounter with God's Holy Spirit that day.

God surely saw in me what I could not see. It probably is my compassion for suffering ones. I have been in most of their circumstances, with physical pain, suffering a broken heart and physical abuse. I remember my physical pain as well as my emotional anguish. Remembering makes me more compassionate with others. The pain of a broken heart was more painful than the pain in my flesh. Yet my calling is deeper than compassion. I get angry with satan for what he does to mankind.

After my healing was complete, I went into homes and ministered to terminally ill people and sat by their bedsides for a week at a time. I went to hospitals and sat with the sick. The first young lady I ministered to in the hospital died unexpectedly in my arms the second day I was there. I was devastated when that happened and I wanted to stop ministering.

The lady's husband said I must never quit. He heard her tell me the night before she died that I had given her the happiest day of her life. I had ministered to her spirit and lifted her so high that she had made that statement. Her peace and joy came as I ministered; she was laughing. What a way to go to Heaven!

Once I spent weeks with a neighbor who had multiple sclerosis (MS). She was too sick to stay alone, so I sat by her bedside daily, until she was strong enough to care for herself. God later healed her of MS.

Since then, she has become a dear friend. She says that I have become like her second mother, and I agree!

There are many wounded ones in need of helping hands, but so few are willing to labor in that ministry. The need is greater than the number of those willing to minister. Some are in life-and-death battles as satan is warring against the saints. But he only wins the battle when God's Word is not faithfully enforced. I have taught many people at home how to win their faith battle.

After five years of praying for the ill in their homes, God called me into full-time evangelistic teaching ministry, as I mentioned previously. I teach healing classes in churches, to instruct people how to speak God's Word until their victory comes.

My greatest desire is to teach people how to gain healing by using God's Word. The Word of God carries His authority and His power as we speak and say it, and that Word destroys diseases. No devil is big enough to defeat a serious child of God who is willing to execute God's Word forcefully on that devil!

My evangelistic teaching job that God gave me has changed from my dread into my greatest joy. My faith is fully in God's ability as I teach people how to receive answers from His infallible Word. God called me to instill faith in His people.

The spiritual warfare techniques, which are taught in the text of this book, are not an automatic guarantee against the enemy's attacks. However, if applied faithfully, they will bring victory to you. I pray that you will be set free by reading this book and by applying God's powerful Word to your circumstance. God's Words are Spiritual, and they enrich our lives as we find and apply them. (See Proverbs 4:20-22.)

There is victory for all who will use the principles that I teach—that is, if they stay focused on God's Word and apply His Words faithfully and forcefully. By exercising our authority that God gave in His Word, we can get our healing manifestation.

Everyone can experience the miracle-working power that comes by executing God's powerful, living Word. God is faithful to perform His Words that we are faithful to state over our problems, pain conditions, and circumstances—if we faithfully obey God's instructions of walking His love walk.

We must walk in total forgiveness, because walking in total forgiveness is God's way and that will please Him and put Him to work in our life. Then there is nothing that He will not do for us because we are delighting ourselves in the Lord's ways, by obeying His Word. He will give us the desires of our heart, according to Psalms 37:4.

God made you a free moral agent and you have a right to choose to go God's way and win; or you have a right to choose to go your own way and fail. If you do not obey God's instructions, then don't blame Him for your failure!

If you want to turn defeat into victory you must choose to come God's way. You *can* leave defeat behind and gain victory as you trust in God and obey His Word! Amen!

Chapter 9

How Healing Operates

Throughout my healing process I searched the Bible for answers. I studied the ministry of Jesus and found it is God's will to heal all who will believe His Word and then execute His Word in faith! Psalms 138:2b (KJV) says, "For Thou hast magnified Thy Word above all Thy Name." Until I knew that much about God's credibility, my enemy devoured me. Knowing Jesus as Savior was not enough to heal my body when lupus struck me.

My church taught that the gift of healing had passed away with the apostles, and the Holy Spirit baptism had passed as well. They cannot prove that doctrine from God's Word. I can prove that it is false information sent by satan. Never believe all that you hear. Instead, get your information from the Bible. Ignorance almost cost me my life. I would have died had I not found God's will in my Bible concerning healing.

God is the same today as He was yesterday (see Heb. 13:8). That means that neither God nor His Word has changed. Therefore, the Holy Ghost and healing are gifts for today. The problem is that many believe the diagnosis of a doctor rather than believing God's Word. They are more carnally minded than spiritually minded—they have a relationship problem with God.

"It is impossible for God to lie..." (Heb. 6:18). He is trustworthy. If people only knew God's character, they would trust and believe His Word. Unbelief stems from a lack of relationship. By fellowshiping with people we learn to trust them. If I made a promise and you did not trust me, I would be deeply hurt. By using the same principle, how do you think God feels if we believe a doctor's bad report over His report?

God's Word overrides all doctors' reports. Therefore, trust that God's Word works, or faith cannot deliver your substance. Check Hebrews 11:6 and see how important your faith is: "But without faith it is impossible to please Him, for he who comes to God must believe that He is, and that He is a rewarder of those who diligently seek Him."

When we diligently seek God, He rewards us for our efforts! Jesus warns us how the thief comes to steal, kill, and destroy. But then He says He came so we may have life, and that we might have life more abundantly. (See John 10:10.) What a contrast between satan's mission and Jesus' mission! If we never receive that statement of fact personally, we are deceived and are unable to receive God's promises. Whom do we believe? Do we believe Jesus, or satan? We each must make this decision!

Romans 14:23 says, "But he who doubts is condemned if he eats, because he does not eat of faith; for whatever is not of faith is sin." Doubting God's Word on any subject is counted as sin! God healed then and still does! See Acts 10:38: "How God anointed Jesus of Nazareth with the Holy Spirit and with power, who went about doing good and healing all who were oppressed by the devil, for God was with Him."

Jesus healed those oppressed by satan back then, and He still will! "Jesus is the same yesterday, today, and forever" (Heb. 13:8). He never changed! Instead, man's doctrine changed the Word and stripped it of its power, making it ineffective!

God's Word Met My Personal Need

The medical profession told me there was no medical cure for lupus. However, I knew there had to be an answer. I searched my Bible for truth, and there I found my answer. I applied it to my case. Now I am in perfect health and have my normal weight back. I have been declared healed from lupus for 16 years. My healing process took from January 1983 until January 1984 to complete.

I am a witness to the fact that God heals today! So you too can be healed by faith in His Word. Jesus said in Matthew 9:29, "According to your faith let it be to you." Believing God's Word is key to receiving His promises. Until we personally know God and believe His Word, we cannot personally trust His report.

"Faith comes by hearing, and hearing by the Word of God" (Rom. 10:17). When our ears hear our mouth speak God's Word continually, then victory will come. The following verses that I used will increase your faith as you apply them faithfully.

Psalms 118:17 says, "I shall not die, but live, and declare the works of the Lord." Isaiah 53:5 states, "But He was wounded for our transgressions, He was bruised for our iniquities; the chastisement for our peace was upon Him, and by His stripes we are healed."

Notice that the word *are* is an ongoing word; it's in the present tense of the "now" realm. Healing faith is "right now"! If we are healed, we say: "I was healed!" "By whose stripes you *were* healed" (1 Pet. 2:24).

I personalized God's Word and said, "By Jesus' stripes I am healed now!" His *were* word is past tense, indicating it is finished. To believe in my soul means *in my mind, my will, and my emotions!* My faith made healing flow into my body. Then joy came and gave strength to my body as Nehemiah 8:10 says, "The joy of the Lord is your strength."

So joy and strength filled me when I trusted God's report! I had felt hopeless before receiving God's Word as a true report. Before then, joy and strength had left. I felt weak and defenseless. I called strength back as I called myself healed, well, and strong. By using God's method of calling things that are not into being surely worked for me, and it can work for you too. My mindset changed, and slowly my strength came back.

If you need healing you must get someone to agree with you and pray by claiming the Scripture in Matthew 18:19: "Again I say to you that if two of you agree on earth concerning anything that they ask, it will be done for them by My Father in Heaven." I have had miracles by standing upon this Scripture. God is faithful to His Word! The agreement prayer is powerful! This is God's faithful promise! As the minister had prayed Matthew 18:19 over me, in my mind I agreed. I stood firmly without wavering upon the promise, and then results came. My faith by our agreement made it happen in my body!

I found a promise that no weapon formed against me prospers. I personalized my Isaiah promise: "No weapon formed against me shall prosper" (Is. 54:17a).

I personalize this verse and place the word *me* where the word *you* was. As sickness is a bad weapon,

I placed a demand on satan. I demanded in Jesus' Name that satan would get his sickness weapon off my body, that Jesus had redeemed me.

I told satan that I was protected by Jesus' Blood and redeemed from enemy curses. I told him that sickness was a curse I would not put up with. As I stated God's Word I cancelled satan's plan! He began backing off as I enforced God's Word. Slowly symptoms disappeared in my body as I used the authority Jesus had promised me in Luke chapter 10: "Behold, I give unto you power to tread on serpents and scorpions, and over all the power of the enemy: and nothing shall by any means hurt you" (Luke 10:19 KJV).

Daily, I stomped my feet and told lupus I was treading on that lupus devil. I said, "Jesus gives me power to tread on lupus devils!" I said, "Lupus, you cannot kill me. Jesus gave me power over all power from my enemy. This lupus enemy must go."

I gave lupus no choice about staying in my body. You must do likewise with cancer, lupus, MS, AIDS, or any other evil attack! Then I claimed a promise of long life: "With long life I will satisfy him, and show him My salvation" (Psalms 91:16).

I knew God would do what He said in His Word. So I said, "I know I shall have a long, healthy life. God is my salvation and He gives restoration to my body today." You must confess the same to get results. I quoted

God's restoration promise that He would restore health and heal my wounds, as stated in Jeremiah 30:17a: "For I will restore health to you and heal you of your wounds, says the Lord."

"I will" is a strong promise. Daily I claimed, "God will heal me!" I said, "God will, oh yes, He will heal me. Jesus, You are healing and restoring my health. You are healing my wounds now. Jesus, I know that you are healing me now, and I know that no good thing will my God withhold from me as I walk uprightly."

I told God that I loved Him and believed His Word would heal me! Then I claimed an Exodus promise that God would not allow this lupus disease to destroy me by quoting the following verse:

"If you diligently heed the voice of the Lord your God and do what is right in His sight, give ear to His commandments and keep all His statutes, I will put none of the diseases on you which I have brought on the Egyptians. For I am the Lord who heals you" (Exodus 15:26).

Notice the word *put* was not properly translated. In the original Greek it was *permit*. This indicated God permitted sickness on the Egyptians. They were His enemies and served false gods. They never honored God though God sent Moses as a witness to prove His mercy to them. So God permitted sickness upon them as they dishonored Him. To disobey is sin. "Therefore, to him who knows to do good and does not do it, to him it is sin" (Jas. 4:17).

Also God allows illness when we fail to properly care for our bodies. Everyone must obey God's health laws. We must also obey God's spiritual laws on forgiveness:

> *"And whenever you stand praying, if you have anything against anyone, forgive him, that your Father in Heaven may also forgive you your trespasses. But if you do not forgive, neither will your Father in Heaven forgive your trespasses"* (Mark 11:25-26).

Forgiving is mandatory, no exceptions! I checked my heart to make sure that I had forgiven all offenders and to see that I no longer carried hurts. I asked God to forgive me for nursing old wounds. God wants us to forget them. I had forgiven, yet I had not forgotten. Satan kept me reminiscing as I had been wounded in my spirit. God wanted to heal my wounds, but my reminiscing was hindering. Dwelling on offenses borders on not forgiving by God's righteous standard! Check God's standard: "For I will forgive their iniquity, and their sin I will remember no more" (Jer. 31:34).

As I searched the Word I saw how God forgave. So must I forgive by leaving hurts behind and forgetting my wounds! God's way to forgive is to stop reminiscing about old offenses! So I chose to forget my old wound. Then I was ready to execute the Word below:

"For assuredly I say to you, whoever says to this mountain, 'Be removed and be cast into the sea,' and does not doubt in his heart, but believes that those things he says will be done, he will have whatever he says. Therefore I say to you, whatever things you ask when you pray, believe that you receive them, and you will have them" (Mark 11:23-24).

When we speak by faith to mountainous problems, we absolutely and surely shall get what we say if we pray and confess without doubting these verses or doubting God's honesty! God is honest! He is trustworthy according to the following Scripture: "God is not a man, that He should lie, nor a son of man, that He should repent. Has He said, and will He not do? Or has He spoken, and will He not make it good?" (Num. 23:19)

God's promises are all true, sure, and reliable: "By two immutable things, in which it is impossible for God to lie, we might have strong consolation, who have fled for refuge to lay hold of the hope set before us" (Heb. 6:18).

By proclaiming God's promises, hope then anchored my thoughts and brought rest into my soul.

Hope kept me from worry and that stabilized and anchored my mind as the following states, "This hope we have as an anchor of the soul, both sure and steadfast, and which enters the Presence behind the veil, where the forerunner has entered for us, even Jesus, having become High Priest forever according to the order of Melchizedek" (Heb. 6:19-20).

Jesus is our High Priest and He has run before us. He now sits at the right hand of the Father, making intercession for us. He makes all our promises from God steadfast and concrete! Make sure to not get an evil heart of unbelief: "Beware, brethren, lest there be in any of you an evil heart of unbelief in departing from the living God" (Heb. 3:12).

So never have an evil heart of unbelief or neglect to confess God's Word over satan's attack. It is vital to confess God's Word so that Jesus as High Priest can plead our case in Heaven's court. Jesus comes into our situation as we confess the Word, then He acts as our High Priest and attorney. "Seeing then that we have a great High Priest who has passed through the Heavens, Jesus the Son of God, let us hold fast our confession" (Heb. 4:14).

As we live by God's instructions we get Him involved. Then we can pray what Jesus said in Matthew's Gospel as stated below:

"Our Father in Heaven, hallowed be Your name. Your kingdom come. Your will be done on

earth as it is in Heaven. Give us this day our daily bread. And forgive us our debts, as we forgive our debtors" (Matthew 6:9-12).

Until I forgot the past, God never sent big blessings. So as I stayed in God's Word 12 months, I forgot the past. My Bible was open before me as I continually consumed the Word. There was life in God's Word. My spirit was hungry to learn of His ways.

In God's Word I found covenant promises. I found direction, correction, hope, peace, joy, strength, trust, and contentment beyond anything I had known. I found that religion now portrays God differently, although God and His Word have never changed.

The promises in God's Word anchored my hope and stabilized my thoughts. My faith and trust began growing by leaps and bounds. God healed my broken heart and made it as though it had never been broken. I was ready to be serious with God for my healing. God always blesses us when we seriously turn to Him.

If we stay sick without receiving healing, we may have buried hurts within our soul. Healings or hurts both start within the soulish realm. Then they manifest as either health or sickness in our body. When our soul heals, our body heals also. A tree limb is no healthier than its root system. So neither is our body any healthier than the emotions of our soulish realm.

God's Word is medicine that cures emotions and brings health and peace to our mind. I found that

Psalms 1:1-3 gave direction, and Mark 11:23-24 gave instructions how to talk to the mountainous problems that satan created in my mind and my life.

My spirit grew strong as I talked to the lupus mountain. I demanded a lupus spirit to leave me. I talked to the wounds satan had inflicted. I admit, it took much effort and commitment on my part. But I stayed diligently faithful through the long ordeal.

The enemy used lying pain symptoms and sleepless nights against me. He planned for me to observe symptoms more than I observed God's Word. He tried to keep them strong on my mind. But I took charge of my mind and cast out his thoughts, keeping my mind focused on God's promises instead.

Satan never successfully wore me down or caused me to stop commanding symptoms to go, although he tried to do this by turning up the pain. He really tried to keep my mind off God's promises. But he lost deception's battle over my mind! If we never seriously take charge of our mind, or take our thoughts captive like Second Corinthians 10:5 instructs, we lose the battle and satan wins!

If we give more attention to a lying pain symptom, or the offense, than we give attention to God's Word, satan will whip us! But if we obey Psalms 1:1-3 and meditate God's Word day and night, our spirit and our soul flourish and prosper. Then we win, as our health grows stronger by obeying God's instructions.

When we deposit God's Word into our spirits, those words flourish, and go out through our bodies. Our emotional realm heals from the words deposited therein. There is enough life and power in God's Word to heal the spirit, soul, and body of any dying person even today. So we must trust all of God's Words and claim them, so then we will get all His blessings! God's Words are our covenant promises, and He makes His promises sure!

First Thessalonians 5:24 says, "He who calls you is faithful, who also will do it." Jesus faithfully performs His Word that we faithfully keep saying. He is a faithful High Priest over His Word. Jesus and His Word both are faithful and they both can bring healing blessings into your sick body today.

Preaching is inspiring and great to lift up our spirits, but after the emotions settle down, what do you know that you can put to practice toward kicking the devil out? I am so grateful that I have had two of the greatest teachers in the world, who have taught me how faith operates. Their names are Dr. Norvel Hayes, and my pastor Dr. James C. Hash. Without the teaching of God's Word we could come up short of faith. Our minds can grasp much more as we study God's laws and His instructions in His Word. His Word truly does enrich our life.

So turn to God's Word; study and search for God with your whole heart by searching His Word. Then when you find your promise, stake your claim and trust God for the answer. Defeated days will drop off, and victory will come to you just as victory came to me when I turned to God with my whole heart!

Chapter 10

God's Word Is Authority

God placed His authority within His Word, and then He gave us authority to speak His Word. Then those spoken words perform as if God Himself uttered them. The amount of His Word we store in our hearts determines the level of authority that we can enforce on satan, as he tries to steal the Word from us by injecting thoughts of fear or defeat. So look out for his trap.

First Peter 5:8 instructs us to "Be sober, be vigilant; because your adversary the devil walks about like a roaring lion, seeking whom he may devour." If we meditate upon fear, we are positioning ourselves to be a prime target for satan's attacks!

Jesus whipped satan and stripped his power. He has no right to destroy God's people unless they meditate upon negative fear reports. Get wise. Use God's Word, as God never blesses ignorance. Meditating on fears or cares takes us outside God's faith zone, into satan's attack zone; while meditating on God's Word activates God's presence and brings us victory!

When we control our thoughts our faith grows stronger. Then our spiritual ignorance cannot cause satan's schemes to make us become his victims. As we meditate on God's Word, that meditation builds a strong faith shield so satan cannot penetrate through, according to Ephesians Chapter 6, in the following verses:

"Finally, my brethren, be strong in the Lord and in the power of His might. Put on the whole armour of God, that ye may be able to stand against the wiles of the devil. For we wrestle not against flesh and blood, but against principalities, against powers, against the rulers of the darkness of this world, against spiritual wickedness in high places" (Ephesians 6:10-12 KJV).

Can you see how satan plots evil schemes against us? These verses show how our faith has an enemy to combat. That is why we must use God's Word, and also use His method for our protection.

"Therefore take up the whole armor of God, that you may be able to withstand in the evil day, and having done all, to stand. Stand therefore, having girded your waist with truth, having put on the breastplate of righteousness, and having shod your feet with the preparation of the gospel of peace; above all, taking the shield of faith with which you will be able to quench all the fiery darts of the wicked one. And take the helmet of salvation, and the sword of the Spirit, which is the Word of God; praying always with all prayer and supplication in the Spirit, being watchful to this end with all perseverance" (Ephesians 6:13-18a).

Satan backs off as we diligently persevere and pray God's Word over our problems. Praying the Word gives us insight into satan's plans, especially if we are terminally ill. As we pray God's Word we stop satan's attacks. God's Word wins because His Word is His will. God hastens to perform His Words that we pray!

When we pray God's Word we allow that Word to bring God's will to pass. The Word transforms our mind, creating faith so we can trust Isaiah 53:5 and First Peter 2:24. Both verses say that by Jesus' stripes we are, and we were, healed! So believe it!

God never breaks covenant with His Word. And His Word is already settled in Heaven. (See Psalms 89:34 and Psalms 119:89.)

Philippians 2:5 says, "Let this mind be in you, which was also in Christ Jesus." Jesus used the Word's authority, so must we! Using God's Word stabilizes thought patterns so that we can be transformed into Christ's image, which is God's will for us.

In order to gain knowledge and learn our authority, we must intimately get to know who Jesus is. John 1:1 says, "In the beginning was the Word, and the Word was with God, and the Word was God." In John 1:10 and John 1:14, we see that Jesus was God incarnate, God in the flesh. He is the second person of the Godhead of the Trinity. He heals sick bodies and forgives sins.

Jesus is co-equal with God and He is the express image of the Father. John 10:30 says, "I and My Father are one." They are one in word, and both Jesus and His Word carry great authority.

In Acts 10:38 Jesus healed all that were oppressed of the devil. In Hebrews 13:8 we read that Jesus is the same yesterday, today, and forever. Jesus never changed the authority of the Word. The doctrine of man has stripped the Word of its power!

Hosea 4:6a says, "My people are destroyed for lack of knowledge." Healing comes from our knowledge of God's nature and by knowing His covenant Word. Until we know and understand the goodness of God's plan, it's difficult to see healing manifest.

God is good and He gives us good gifts. Satan gives bad gifts such as sickness, pain, sorrow or death to those without the knowledge of the authority they would have by enforcing God's Word on satan. God is good; His goodness is proved by this verse: "Every good gift and every perfect gift is from above, and comes down from the Father of lights, with whom there is no variation or shadow of turning" (Jas. 1:17).

Psalms 103:3 says, "[God] forgives all your iniquities [and] heals all your diseases." Our faith grows if we know the goodness of God and learn about His credibility. As we learn and understand the immutability of God's love nature our authority in His Word will increase, and then faith starts working.

Jesus implied in Matthew 15:26 that healing is the children's bread. Our authority on healing is found in God's Word. Jesus paid an awesome price for our healing with stripes on His back. Our part is to believe, trust, and accept our healing by faith in that report. Again I say, victory is found in God's atonement promise in Isaiah 53:5, and also in First Peter 2:24. Amen!

We obtain healing the same way that we obtained salvation, by believing in our heart and confessing God's report with our mouth. (See Romans 10:9-10.) By repeating God's Word over and over, faith in the Word registers in our hearts. God's Word gives life to our souls, then deposits it to our bodies. Healing comes unless we waver from meditating on His Word. Neglect allows satan to steal it from our mouth and our heart.

Proverbs 6:2 warns not to be snared by our words. Psalms 107:20a says, "He sent His Word and healed them." According to God's Word, sickness leaves as we boldly declare or say God's Word with authority as stated in Mark 11:23. God's Word brings healing into our body if we are steadfast, without doubting in our heart. Faith delivers our desires according to the Word!

John 15:7 says, "If you abide in Me, and My Words abide in you, you will ask what you desire, and it shall be done for you." This indicates His Word abiding within us brings the boldness to ask or demand and then to receive from that Word. To get blessings on a large scale we must stay obedient! Then we can have the petition that we desire, according to First John 5:14-15: "Now this is the confidence that we have in Him, that if we ask anything according to His will, He hears us. And if we know that He hears us, whatever we ask, we know that we have the petitions that we have asked of Him."

How to Get Faith to Work

By the authority of God's Word, He will answer when our words agree with His will within His Word. So ask for healing, then declare His Word! Speaking God's Word releases Him to perform! Jeremiah 1:12b (KJV), "For I will hasten My Word to perform it." Speaking God's Word ignites and activates the power and authority contained within His Word. So say, "I am being healed by Jesus' stripes, and I am being healed right now!"

Never say, "I am going to be healed." Instead, say, "According to God's report in Isaiah 53:5, Jesus has paid for my healing and I accept my healing now! I believe God's report!"

God is good! Psalms 84:11b says, "No good thing will He withhold from those who walk uprightly." God never denies our healing if we walk His way, free from sin, declaring His Word.

Though we use our authority and stand on the Word, we cannot get full results from our stand unless we take care of our health with proper nutrition, exercise, rest, and sleep. Our authority is useless until we are obedient to all God's laws. In addition to the physical, there are mental, emotional, and spiritual reasons for illness. And reasons can override physical health care and stop our authority. The following revised paragraphs were taken from my healing booklet I wrote in 1991.

Some Causes of Illness

Reason 1: *Discouragement* is the number one tool of satan. It leads to disappointment and then disappointment leads to sorrow. Discouragement is a big tool that satan uses to stop our faith and our fellowship with God. We must pray and worship and praise God. This causes satan to flee. Then our spirit can be lifted into peace and joy. If possible, we must go to the one who offended us and make things right. If we stay discouraged without pulling out of it, reason two will begin.

Reason 2: *Depression* then sets in if we fail to overcome discouragement. Depression may lead us into reason number three.

Reason 3: *Unforgiveness* creates a frame of mind that causes every cell in our body to malfunction. This leads to many illnesses. If we find ourselves in this category, we must obey Ephesians 4:26b, "Do not let the sun go down on your wrath." God requires our total forgiveness so illness cannot strike us.

Reason 4: *Loss of Joy* creates a negative atmosphere. Illness thrives on negative words. Then we let joy slip; we slump and are emotionally weak and defenseless. Joyfulness is a choice we must make. Philippians 4:4 says, "Rejoice in the Lord always. Again I will say, rejoice!" Nehemiah 8:10b says, "The joy of the Lord is your strength." Our defense is our joy!

Reason 5: *Lacking commitment to God's Spiritual matters* can hinder our faith walk. Matthew 6:33 says, "But seek first the kingdom of God and His righteousness, and all these things shall be added to you." Peace and physical well being comes by obeying God's laws. On the other hand, preoccupation with worldly material gains, gambling, drinking, immoral sex, gluttony, or gossip separates us from God. These things hinder faith and stop our prayers. Then we remain weak and feel condemned before God.

Reason 6: *Debts undermine our health.* Being deep in debt may cause a sense of unworthiness. We must take care of our debts and seek help to develop a plan to get out of debt. We must always tithe by giving God His tenth first. Then we must be willing to share with the poor and needy as Jesus commanded.

Reason 7: *Fear and anxiety* are two spirits that will remove God's protection. Without protection, we cannot continue our healing process. Second Timothy 1:7 says, "For God has not given us a spirit of fear, but of power and of love and of a sound mind." To get rid of those spirits of fear and anxiety, we must daily fellowship and have a relationship with God. Then those two spirits will leave and not be likely to return.

If fear and anxiety still bother our mind, we must resist the temptation to entertain them. They are spirits from satan. Command them to flee in Jesus' Name. They have to obey. Faith drives them out as faith builds us up. A fear spirit knocks us down.

Reason 8: *Failure to walk in love* is the root cause for all illness. If we are walking a love walk, we are keeping God's commandments. If we love our neighbor we cannot covet his possessions; instead we act in kindness like we want him to act. Then we obey the love commandments in Matthew as written below:

Our Love Commandments

"You shall love the Lord your God with all your heart, with all your soul, and with all your mind." This is the first and great commandment. And the second is like it: "You shall love your neighbor as yourself. On these two commandments hang all the Law and the Prophets" (Matthew 22:37-40).

Other Vital Steps Toward Healing

If we need healing we may have someone who is a strong believer to anoint us with oil and pray according to James 5:14-15a: "Is anyone among you sick? Let him call for the elders of the church, and let them pray over him, anointing him with oil in the name of the Lord. And the prayer of faith will save the sick, and the Lord will raise him up."

How to Minister Healing to the Sick

The one ministering must be living free from sin, so he can curse infirmities in Jesus' Name, and lay hands on them and pray. Mark 16:18 can be paraphrased, "They lay hands on the sick, and they recover." According to Hebrews 6:12 we then are recovering!

We must obey Matthew 5:44 and keep a right relationship with God by fellowshiping, thanking, and worshiping Him daily. Also, our relationship with people is vital. We must forgive our enemies and pray for those who hate us as well. Then adopt a daily Bible reading plan and be consistent.

Tame Your Tongue

We must tame our tongue and not voice how badly we feel. Instead, we need to state that we are recovering and that God is healing us according to His Word. "Faith comes by hearing, and hearing by the Word of God" (Rom. 10:17). We should read the Word aloud whenever possible. This allows faith to build in our heart as we hear God's Word stated. We must be careful what we say. Proverbs warns that death can result from our words.

If doctors or nurses are needed, it is important that we choose those who will encourage the sick. Encouragement is not phony enthusiasm, but it gives strength and helps the afflicted. It will lift their spirits and hasten their recovery.

All visitors or companions must demonstrate a gentle, loving spirit. The sick ones' faith can be strengthened, and they can be encouraged toward healing as we pray and praise God and rejoice over them. Stay away from gloomy, pessimistic, negative people. Bad spirits and attitudes can transfer to the sick.

Pray the Answer Instead of the Problem

We are not to pray the problem! Never say, "Lord I feel so sick, please take away the pain in my body!"

Instead, we pray the Word. According to Matthew 18:18, we can loose assignments against us. Say, "I believe Jesus redeems, heals and restores!"

We must keep thanking God for our healing even though it may not have manifested yet. Believe First Peter 2:24, as this truly is God's accurate Word. What God has declared in His Word we must declare. God then brings it to pass if we obey Mark 11:23 by talking to our mountainous problems, and if we do not doubt the authority of God's Words that we are declaring!

Condemnation or Justification

Matthew 12:37 says, "For by your words you will be justified, and by your words you will be condemned." Jesus never came to condemn us. (See John 3:17.) Our own words condemn us! We must be careful of each word we speak and never say anything negative. Never claim sickness. Instead, say, "Jesus is healing me now. By His stripes I'm being healed and I'm recovering now."

We cannot allow satan to tempt us to talk of our attacks. As we talk the attack, we get death. Proverbs proves that words give life or inflict death. Proverbs 18:21 says, "Death and life are in the power of the tongue." So be careful of each word you say. Words are vital, as Matthew 12:36 warns that we give account of every idle word we say. Our world is framed by words.

We turn circumstances by stating First Peter 2:24 and by obeying Mark 11:23. We can confidently say,

"By the stripes of Jesus I am healed! This mountain of illness will obey my command and leave my body in Jesus' Name!" On the authority of God's Word, sickness leaves as we keep saying and demanding it to go. In Jesus' Name we can have what God says. He designed our body to obey our command, so that we can change circumstances!

Always Avoid Strife

We must avoid strife with our companion, children, family, and friends. Healing never manifests when strife is present. We must create an atmosphere where the Spirit of God can operate. God never comes near strife. Faith operates as we walk in a spirit of love and forgiveness. This is the law that God operates through. By walking God's way, we can be healed!

Galatians 5:6 tells us that faith works by love. If there is no love abiding in you, then, there is no faith working for you! There are no exceptions to this rule! I know people who hold offense and anger, and who will not forgive. They are unwilling to forget offenses, so their healing will never manifest.

Forgiveness is a strong key to receiving from God. Mark 11:25-26 proves that God requires total forgiveness! We have no choice in this matter of walking in love and forgiveness. This is the walk Jesus took as He walked to Calvary. He told us to follow Him, so we must obey His command. (See John 1:43.) Jesus crucified His flesh before going to Calvary. Let us crucify our flesh daily and follow His example. Then our faith can operate!

Authority Is Useless Until Law Is Enforced

We must enforce God's law on satan. Jesus gave us power and authority to use the Word on satan. Jesus said that all power was given to Him in both Heaven and earth. (See Matthew 28:18.) In Luke 9:1 and 10:19, Jesus delegated power and authority to His followers. All believing followers can pray and get results!

We are His disciples, so we must assume responsibility and cast out the tormenting spirits that attack our minds and bodies. We must defend our covenant promises and guard our inheritance, and not allow satan to steal our blessings! Jesus delegated us power to use on satan. We must use that power or be defeated!

Never allow satan to tempt you to move into fear. Instead, always stay in faith! Jesus laid the law down on satan, but He left it up to us to enforce the law and demand that satan get out. Use Jesus' Blood for protection, as satan cannot attack through the Blood. We are covenant children. Healing is our bread. Enforce the Word on satan; pray, worship God, and stay strong!

God is our defense and we are protected as we stay in the secret place of the Most High. (See Psalms 91.) Jesus defeated satan and paid our debt by His death and resurrection. He then gave us an inheritance. As delegated caretakers, we must stay on guard. Satan always tries to steal our inheritance from us!

Mark chapter 16 tells us to go into the world and preach the Gospel, cast out devils, and lay hands on the sick and they shall recover. (See Mark 16:15-18.) When we enforce God's Word, demons tremble. They know the authority of God's Word better than most people know the authority of using God's Word! When we use the authority of God's Word, He brings those words to pass. God makes His Word good if we state it: "God is not a man that He should lie, nor a son of man, that He should repent. Has He said, and will He not do? Or has He spoken and will He not make it good?" (Num. 23:19)

So we must trust God for healing, as well as for salvation!

Isaiah 40:8 says, "But the Word of our God stands forever." We can stand forever by firmly planting ourselves on God's Word no matter what doctors may say about our condition!

We reap from every word we give a voice to say. As my words conformed to God's will within His Word, He then performed His Word. (See Jeremiah 1:12.) To say God's Word instead of a doctor's report justifies us. God makes sure we don't make liars of ourselves when we say His Words. My words justify me to overcome!

Our Words Justify Us to Overcome

"Let God be true but every man a liar. As it is written: That you may be justified in your words and may overcome when you are judged" (Rom. 3:4).

Negative Words Versus Positive Words

Positive words activate God's power and then He performs them, while negative words activate satan's power so he performs them. So enforce God's Word over a doctor's bad report! Proverbs 18:20 says we will eat fruit from our words. We must make our words sweet, as we all eat fruit from our words sooner or later.

God's spoken Word gave power to heal my body as it germinated my faith seed. The authority in the Word set my healing in motion! (See Psalms 107:20.) By using the authority of God's Word, lupus left me, because my mind conformed to His Word. As your mind conforms to His Word, He will heal you too!

Chapter 11

Never Let Satan Steal Your Joy

Until we combine faith, hope, and joy, we cannot reach our healing goal because victory depends upon this entire combination. By staying filled with this combination, God takes notice that we are resting in the promises of His Word.

Godly Hope Enables Us to Abound

Romans 15:13 says, "Now may the God of hope fill you with all joy and peace in believing, that you may abound in hope by the power of the Holy Spirit."

Godly Hope Is a Fuel Booster

Hope acts as fuel, boosting faith's rocket off the launching pad. Hope also needs joy to kick in with its fuel to keep the faith rocket on course. Without joy, the rocket of faith will fail and never reach its goal.

Joyfulness and rejoicing both hasten victory. If we are happy, we are building good cells. If we are sad, they become depleted. So we must thank God for joy before we feel like rejoicing, as a thankful heart creates joy to hasten His answers.

Jeremiah 31:13b says, "I will turn their mourning to joy, will comfort them, and make them rejoice rather than sorrow." Our rejoicing will expel sorrows and boost our spirits higher.

Romans 14:17 says, "For the kingdom of God is not eating and drinking, but righteousness and peace and joy in the Holy Spirit." My key to staying joyful is by believing and trusting God's Word. Then sorrow turns to gladness, and faith and peace reward me with joy. "Your joy no one will take from you" (Jn. 16:22b).

Maintaining our joy is one key to receiving God's promises. Joy is vital in helping us stay peaceful and calm. During my lupus attack, I lived in Psalms 23. I rested when it seemed like all hell raged around me. I continually stayed peaceful by relying on God's promises. My joyful and peaceful spirit proved that my trust remained in God's promises.

It might not seem possible, but we can lie down in green pastures as our enemies surround us. (See Psalms 23.) This kind of peace produces joy unspeakable in our soulish realm. A joyful believer proves

God's promises and gains his substance as evidence. Joyfulness confuses satan and delays his evil attacks.

"Great peace have those who love Your law, and nothing causes them to stumble" (Ps. 119:165). If we honor God's Word, we retain peace. Then satan loses his ability to stop our joyfulness by invading our peace with anger, offenses, or worry.

Beware how satan can use deception to steal joyfulness from your heart. He is a professional con artist who is a very good thief. All he has to do is give us pain or a bad thought, and we run to a doctor to find out what is wrong! If a doctor gives us bad news, we forget Isaiah 53:5, and end up taking a doctor's report as truth. We become sorrowful and forget that by Jesus' stripes we were healed two thousand years ago at Calvary. We then lose our faith, hope, and joy, and forget God's honest report.

Do you see how slyly satan steals our peace and joy? When joy is gone, we are weak and defenseless. Satan did this to me when my doctor said I had lupus. When I received that bad lupus report, satan told me to give up and quit. Then he said that I was not going to make it. He said, "Stop trying, as no one has been healed of lupus. God does not heal, especially those who are diagnosed as medically incurable."

I questioned that report! I had been taught that God was always good. But I did not know God's healing covenant plan back then. Satan's clever agenda was to lure me into sorrow and fear. His plan was to steal my joy so that he could make me give up my hope and my faith in God's promises.

However, two years after my bad report, I heard God's true report. I believed the good news of God's Word and continued trusting, although pain and symptoms remained. I had already survived liver and kidney failure, plus four years of pain when I first heard of God's healing report. I kept my hopes that God would touch me. So I gladly accepted healing the first time I heard God's healing report. Joyfulness flooded my soul.

Take notice, when you surrender your mind to bad news, that you become tired and weak. Nehemiah 8:10b: "The joy of the Lord is your strength." Satan knows this fact so he looks for ways to steal our joy. We must get wise to his schemes and stop surrendering our joy. The loss of joy causes our strength to vanish and then we lose faith for our healing battle.

The Importance of Joy and Gladness

"Because you did not serve the Lord your God with joy and gladness of heart, for the abundance of everything, therefore you shall serve your enemies, whom the Lord will send against you, in hunger, in thirst, in nakedness, and in need of everything" (Deuteronomy 28:47-48b).

According to the previous verses, we can never please God without retaining joy. We must stay joyful and thankful for our blessings instead of confessing problems! It's important to serve God with joyfulness, as a joyful heart brings blessings.

A couple of years ago, I was ministering and teaching about spiritual battles in the enemy's territory. Satan did not like it so he launched a big attack to steal my joyfulness. I was teaching healing classes to the terminally ill at Dr. Norvel Hayes's church, and had just finished with a session on the importance of retaining joy. Upon arriving home, I learned that two close friends had died and were buried while I was gone.

Two days later my pet dog was killed. For a couple of days my joy left and I was overcome with sorrow and grief. Then the Holy Spirit said to me, "Remember last week you taught those people the importance of retaining joy!" Like a flash I saw how cleverly satan had stolen my joy. I realized this was another one of his big schemes. So I said, "Satan, you will never steal my peace and joy and leave me weak and defenseless again. I will fight a big faith battle and keep my joy."

I am determined to live above my circumstances. God's Word gives joy no matter what comes my way. God is with me always and behind every cloud the sun is shining brightly.

Two months after that big attack, I had a car wreck. Though my car was totaled, I did not get a scratch. I kept my joy and cast the care of my lost car on the Lord and called Him my provider. I worshiped God daily and He supplied me with another car two months later. It was not easy keeping my joy as I observed my badly crushed car. My mind was determined to not allow satan to steal my joy again no matter what he did!

If you are going through a trial, cheer up! There is always victory after the battle if you do not throw in the towel and quit! Satan may try you sorely, but faith can win that battle. Your mind must stay set with peace and joy from God's Word. Trials are not easy, but without them you never receive a testimony. Never be downhearted in testing! Stay filled with joy knowing your testimony comes after you prove that you will not let satan steal your joy. Joy is one big key to victory!

On the other hand, faith is your shield against fear. Faith keeps the fear door closed so satan cannot enter. If you fall into fear, you stop faith's operation. Fear can rob joy from our heart and leave us defenseless against satanic attacks.

Other overcoming keys are alertness and watchfulness. Again, I paraphrase John 10:10, "The thief comes to steal, to kill, and to destroy." Then after the thief, Jesus said in the latter part of John 10:10, "I have come that they may have life, and that they may have it more abundantly." Praise be to Jesus!

Our hearts should be filled with joy to know that Jesus can give us abundant life in spite of the thief. God's report can bring hope, faith, and joy. With these three virtues we have the key, the lock, and the doorway to victory. Yet, we must keep joy and faith posted on duty at the door of our heart at all times. Strong faith never opens a door to satan's evil fear spirit.

"Rejoice in the Lord always. Again I will say, rejoice!" (Phil. 4:4) Rejoicing is difficult until we know God intimately and thereby rely on His Word. Intimacy with God comes from quality time spent in prayer, the Word, worship, and praise. Building fellowship with God in a time of storm is hard to do, but it is possible if we sincerely seek His fellowship.

We can get acquainted with God by joyfully meditating on His Word. Victory is attained as our trust grows stronger. Hebrews 6:18 tells us it is impossible for God to lie. We can believe God's report and live, or we can choose not to believe His report and die. God honors faith, so decide to believe Him!

Doctors may say that we are not going to live. They are not lying but stating a truth from a medical perspective. However, that report doesn't have to be fulfilled, because there is a higher report that erases a doctor's report. Stating God's Word accomplishes the healing God planned. Back when I spoke His Word over lupus symptoms, my physical condition improved.

Satan backed away and 12 months later I was completely well.

The centurion told Jesus, "Lord speak the word only, and my servant will be healed" (Matt. 8:8). Jesus said in response to the centurion's faith, "I have not found so great faith, no, not in Israel" (Matt. 8:10b KJV). We get God's attention by stating His Word over the doctor's report. So never magnify satan's symptoms above God's Word by speaking them. Instead, we must magnify God's Word and use our faith to stay joyful.

God Has Sworn and His Word Stands

"The Lord of hosts has sworn, saying, 'Surely, as I have thought, so it shall come to pass, and as I have purposed, so it shall stand' " (Is. 14:24).

Paraphrasing Our Covenant

First Chronicles 16:15-17 says "Remember His covenant forever, the word which He commanded, for a thousand generations, the covenant which He made with Abraham, and His oath to Isaac, and confirmed it to Jacob for a statute, to Israel for an everlasting covenant."

God's Word Overrides Other Reports

God holds His Word above His Name. (See Psalms 138:2.) Our joy shows God that we trust His credibility.

Psalms 103:2-5 says that God forgives all of our iniquities and sins. He heals all our diseases. He redeems our life from destruction. He crowns our life with loving kindness and tender mercies. He satisfies our mouth with good things so our youth is renewed like an eagle. This illustrates the nature of God's covenant.

God rewarded me with good health as I quoted His Word day by day. I still remain healthy 16 years after quoting His promises. Though I was then in the worst of my attack, I spoke God's Word faithfully, and by speaking changed my mind to agree with God's Word. He rewarded me with healing in both my soul and body.

God's Mercy Is Everlasting

"The mercy of the Lord is from everlasting to everlasting on those who fear Him, and His righteousness to children's children. . . . Bless the Lord, you His angels, who excel in strength, who do His Word, heeding the voice of His Word" (Psalms 103:17, 20).

The way to get angels involved is to voice God's Word, then our angels will heed to the voice of that Word, as they are ministering spirits that assist God's covenant people. Our angels only listen for God's Word to be spoken. Always remember, as we speak God's Word our angels are working for us.

Matthew 12:34b says, "For out of the abundance of the heart the mouth speaks." Our words prove our heart's content, as our heart is where God's Word is stored. According to Jesus, our heart is as a holding chest where knowledge is stored. Our outcome relies on good knowledge or bad information!

Satan Never Defeats One With a "No Defeat" Attitude

If our hearts contain an abundance of God's Word, His Word comes out of our mouth and makes us joyfully overcome. Isaiah 55:11 says that God's Word will not return unto Him void. By saying His Word, that word accomplishes His planned purpose!

Psalms 107:20 says, "He sent His Word and healed them." Why not use God's Word for personal healing? His Words work as we speak them aloud. Our words must be spoken to accomplish results. Satan cannot read thoughts, so he listens intently to our words. Let's keep our words in agreement with God's Word.

I canceled my death sentence by using God's Word. You can cancel yours if you speak God's Word with faith in God's ability. God never wears a watch, nor does He put us in a future time zone. Never set future dates for healing, as faith performs in the present tense. Only the "now" faith produces results!

James 1:3-4 says, "The testing of your faith produces patience. But let patience have its perfect work, that you may be perfect and complete, lacking nothing."

Luke 21:19 says, "By your patience possess your souls." Either we pass God's faith test or we cannot receive big blessings like stopping death sentences. To pass His faith test we must keep patience, joy, peace, and a full expectation that He will fulfill His promises. Abraham was fully persuaded of God's honesty. So stay persuaded like Abraham! (See Romans 4:16-24.)

Bad news never changes God's report because His Word is forever settled in Heaven. Amen! (See Psalms 119:89.)

"If we are faithless, He remains faithful; He cannot deny Himself" (2 Tim. 2:13). God cannot deny His Word. He is faithful whether you believe or do not believe His Word. People will lie, but "it is impossible for God to lie..." (Heb. 6:18). God is absolutely trustworthy. We can depend on His Word!

Though circumstances look bad, keep on stating God's Word. God performs the Word that we say if we stay in faith and keep our trust in Him. When we trust His Word, that trust keeps our hearts joyful and contented and can stop fear and doubt!

"Let us hold fast the confession of our hope without wavering, for He who promised is faithful" (Heb. 10:23). Knowing that God is faithful should surely make us joyful!

Lamentations 3:22-23, "Through the Lord's mercies we are not consumed, because His compassions fail not. They are new every morning; great is Your faithfulness." Thankfulness turned my emotions so peace remained my companion. Though a fear spirit tried, it never stole my peace. My mind stabilized, trusting God.

"Yea, though I walk through the valley of the shadow of death, I will fear no evil; for You are with me; Your rod and Your staff, they comfort me" (Ps. 23:4). Praise God that "No weapon formed against [us] shall prosper" (Is. 54:17a).

A happy countenance upon our faces will show the world that we trust God. But when our actions show sadness, fear, or downheartedness, we then prove we don't trust God. Sorrowfulness proves disrespect for God's report. Our faith in God's ability generates enough joy to help us win our faith battle!

"Let patience have its perfect work" (Jas. 1:4). Patience and peace supply faith with its needed joy. Satan knows that if our patience is short he can steal our joy. Without joy we are weak and have no defense when satan attacks. "...You have heard of the patience of Job . . ." (Jas. 5:11 KJV). Job got enough trust with his patience, and then satan stopped his attack. And then I suppose Job's joy increased his ability to win!

Satan tried to steal Job's patience so that he could get his joy. And satan still schemes how to get our patience and joy as well. The length and quality of our life is measured by the amount of patience and joy we keep. Having patience with faith in God's ability will give us peace, so that our joy increases!

"A merry heart does good, like medicine, but a broken spirit dries the bones" (Prov. 17:22). Do you have the medicine of a merry heart today? If not, then shout loudly and tell satan to leave in Jesus' Name! Command him to go, so you can get back your joy. In Jesus' Name, satan obeys us if we are not living in sin, or we do not doubt the authority of God's Word.

I never allowed satan to show me visions of death. Instead, I had visions of life and health by meditating on God's report. The image that God's Word printed on my mind stopped satan's plan. When I had lupus, I often awakened at night in great pain. Then satan would put bad thoughts into my mind, but I cast them out quickly without entertaining those suggestions.

I said, "Satan, God's Word says that I am healed by Jesus' stripes, so that means I am healed. Satan, you will never deceive or kill me with lupus or any dreaded disease. I will live and not die because I stand firmly on God's Word that stands forever. According to Isaiah 40:8, the Word of God will stand forever. I know that my healing definitely will stand the test of time. Therefore, I stand on the Word that stands forever; God is always faithful to His Word that I stand on."

Hebrews 6:12, ". . . Through faith and patience [we] inherit the promise." Inheritances aren't always obtained instantly. We must have patience to overcome trials in order to grow in faith and get the inheritance Jesus gave us. Patience must be added to faith to bring our inheritance more quickly. So keep them both!

Unless we have wisdom from God's Word, we will stay in satan's trap without controlling emotions and thoughts. When circumstances dictate our thought patterns our faith will get stalled, and then satan can control our future. Faith in God's Word must not waver, though it rains, or the sun shines.

We may choose to rejoice and live in God's presence, or choose not to rejoice and stay in satan's bondage. Joyfulness builds a wall of protection so that satan cannot devour us. Our praise brings God's presence. Then God abides in our praises. (See Psalms 22:3.) As God draws near, satan flees!

"God...calls those things which do not exist as though they did" (Rom. 4:17b). The wonderful part about His method is that things obey Him. We can do likewise and call things that we desire into being. (See Mark 11:23.) This is the method that God used in Genesis chapter 1, when He called things into being.

I was overjoyed to know that my body could be healed by God's method of calling my health back. I rejoiced and released God to fight my faith battle. "With him is an arm of flesh; but with us is the Lord our God, to help us and to fight our battles" (2 Chron. 32:8). God is greater than satan's battle, so faith eliminated my doubts! God's methods gave peace and joy, stabilizing emotions and erasing sorrows in my soul.

Unless we let God's Word tame our emotions, they can be like a wild horse. Satan knows that by speaking

God's Word we can get answers. So he tries to stop us from speaking the Word. "A man has joy by the answer of his mouth, and a word spoken in due season, how good it is!" (Prov. 15:23) Satan cannot defeat those who answer him with God's Word, especially if they add patience and joy with God's Word!

So beware! If satan steals your joy he can defeat you! If your joy is slipping away and you feel down-hearted and blue, go read my message. Try to correct things, or better yet, give it to Jesus and let Him carry the burden that stole your joy. Leave it with God; let Him carry the load that you cannot carry!

Some people have come into my prayer line wanting God to heal them, yet they were unwilling to let go of an offense. God could not heal them until they let go of the offense. As they forgave, healing came quickly. If that is your problem, then which would you rather carry, your healing or the offense? We cannot have both at one time. Mark 11:25-26 outlines God's doctrine of forgiveness that we all must practice!

If you want healing and you have been offended, then you have no choice but to forgive. Just know that satan deceived the one who wronged you. That person needs your prayers for God's forgiveness. Jesus forgave those who nailed Him to the Cross as He took our place. Follow His example and forgive. The act of forgiving offenders fills your heart with peace and contentment, enabling your heart to retain the joy of the

Lord. Then you will have enough joy to turn your defeat into victory! Amen!

Chapter 12

Faith Requires Corresponding Action

There is power in words that we say. There is power to heal or to kill. Speaking words into the air brings results. So proclaim loudly, "I am healed; I'm healed now!" Faith is useless until it's anointed with action. (See James 2:17-18.) Faith grows by reading and seeking truth from God's Word, praying and using God's Word, witnessing or having anointed ones fellowship.

Romans 10:17, "Faith comes by hearing, and hearing by the Word of God." Our ears must hear ourselves speak God's Word. This is doing, agreeing with, and obeying God's Word. If we do not obey the Word, we are deceived. By speaking God's Word, we open our hearts and minds for greater blessings. James 1:22 says, "But be doers of the Word, and not hearers only, deceiving yourselves." We prove that we trust or agree with God's Word by saying God's Word instead of talking about how big problems are!

Confessions Must Never Waver

"But let him ask in faith, with no doubting, for he who doubts is like a wave of the sea driven and tossed by the wind. For let not that man suppose that he will receive anything from the Lord; he is a double-minded man, unstable in all his ways" (Jas. 1:6-8).

Don't allow feelings to sway confessions! Don't say today that you are healed, then tomorrow say that you are not so sure, because of pain! Confessions must be that we are healed today and still healed tomorrow, pain or no pain! According to God's Word we still are. Don't allow satan to talk away healing.

Second Corinthians 5:7 says, "For we walk by faith, not by sight." This means we are not swayed by feelings. If we trust God's Word, we never regard pain in our body to the point that we stop trusting and confessing God's Word over the symptoms!

"For whatever is not of faith is sin" (Rom. 14:23). According to this verse, if we are not in faith we are in sin. If we know God on a personal basis, we will trust Him. "You will keep Him in perfect peace, whose mind is stayed on You, because he trusts in

You" (Is. 26:3). Trusting God's Word is faith! Without trusting God's Word our faith is worthless.

When our minds remain upon God He gives us peace. That peace gives confidence and rest, for we know that God gives what He promises! That cannot be true if our mind dwells upon the doctor's negative reports that are contrary to God's promises.

God Seeks out People With Faith and Rewards Them

"For the eyes of the Lord run to and fro throughout the whole earth, to show Himself strong on behalf of those whose heart is loyal to Him" (2 Chron. 16:9).

We attract God's attention as we keep faithfully trusting His Word and trusting His ability to perform His promises!

God's Grace Toward Us

Romans 6:14, "For sin shall not have dominion over you, for you are not under law but under grace." God extended His mercy and grace to us, but that doesn't give us a license for sinning, or for excusing willful sin! To stop sinning, our hearts must be cleansed and purged from sin by the Blood of Jesus.

God counts unbelief as sin so we must guard against it. Let us find God, and teach others His wonderful ways. We need His unmerited favor and grace. We don't deserve it, and we haven't earned it. There is no righteousness in our flesh! Our righteousness is as filthy rags. (See Isaiah 64:6.) Flesh has nothing to boast of but God's mercy, His love and His grace!

Jesus extended His love, righteousness, forgiveness, and mercy to us; we must extend the same to others. God forgave us while we were yet undeserving sinners. We must follow His example and extend love, mercy, and forgiveness God's way. There is no exception to the rule. Jesus is a true example of love. He died to His fleshly desires before walking the hill to Calvary.

Jesus Fulfilled the Law

"Do not think that I came to destroy the Law or the Prophets. I did not come to destroy but to fulfill" (Matt. 5:17). His love fulfilled the righteous demand of God's Law. He laid His life down for us though we were not deserving of that love. He extended unmerited grace to all those fallen in sin.

According to Hebrews 8:6-7, Jesus fulfilled the law that man could not keep as He took our place, giving us a better covenant. Our new covenant that Jesus purchased on Calvary is based upon our love relationship with God, and our love walk with man. Walking a love walk fulfills His love commandment.

Romans 13:8, "Owe no one anything except to love one another, for he who loves another has fulfilled the law." Romans 13:10a, "Love does no harm to a neighbor." If love works in our hearts, we love others. Loving hearts cannot stop loving, as that is God's nature on display, proving we are His children!

How to Get God's Favor

One way to get God's favor is to extend love to others. Walking a love walk will activate faith and enable faith to work. Galatians says faith works by love. (See Galatians 5:6.)

Forgiveness Is Mandatory

"And whenever you stand praying, if you have anything against anyone, forgive him, that your Father in Heaven may also forgive you your trespasses. But if you do not forgive, neither will your Father in Heaven forgive your trespasses" (Mark 11:25-26).

This is not a suggestion, but a commandment. We must forgive those who offend us, whether they are big or small offenses.

Love Is the Way

"But I say to you, love your enemies, bless those who curse you, do good to those who hate you and pray for those who spitefully use you and persecute you" (Matt. 5:44).

Forgiveness Is God's Law

Unless we walk by love we never receive God's forgiveness. He gave no option but to obey His forgiveness and love laws. "He who says he is in the light, and hates his brother, is in darkness until now" (1 John 2:9).

The Word says if we hate someone, we are in darkness and do not have eternal life in us. We must check our love walk and see if it measures up to God's love law. Faith never works when we are angry or upset. Walking a love walk helps us overcome the fleshly nature of anger and retaliation. Then our love walk pleases God, and then we will gain His greater blessings.

The following virtues help create a faith-filled love walk, enable us to get healed, and help us maintain healing.

This Is God's Requirement

1. Humility and repentance
2. Obedience to the Word
3. Forgiveness
4. Patience and endurance
5. Trustworthiness
6. Steadfastness and faithfulness
7. Kindness
8. Never taking offense

Get Rid of Anger and Unforgiveness

"Be angry, and do not sin: do not let the sun go down on your wrath" (Eph. 4:26). The Amplified Bible says, "When angry, do not sin; do not ever let your wrath (your exasperation, your fury or indignation) last until the sun goes down." Do not speak or act in anger; back off. Be careful! "A soft answer turns away wrath" (Prov. 15:1). Never speak harshly!

We must always allow anger to cool down. If someone has wronged us, we are to forgive the offender before the sun goes down. Jesus knew that anger would pull us out from God's Spiritual covering, and would thereby leave us unprotected and subject to the attacks that satan desires to inflict upon us.

The Fruit of the Spirit

"But the fruit of the Spirit is love, joy, peace, long-suffering, kindness, goodness, faithfulness, gentleness, self-control" (Gal. 5:22). If we walk in the fruit of God's Spirit we are not under condemnation, as we are covered and protected by God. And we surely do need His covering!

Obedience Keeps Us Protected

"If you diligently heed the voice of the Lord your God and do what is right in His sight, give ear to His commandments and keep all His statutes, I will put none of the diseases on you which I brought on the Egyptians. For I am the Lord who heals you" (Exodus 15:26). God never said to kill; He said He heals!

We Must Execute God's Word

Although we walk by God's law, illness sometimes may come. But God never allows the illness to remain *if* we execute His Word and walk in love. We can say, "Satan, get your hands off me. I am walking in love and you cannot harm me. I walk in God's covenant protection. I will not fear you. I resist you in Jesus' Name. I am protected by God's infallible Word, therefore you will leave me now!"

We Need Wisdom

Wisdom is to know that *if* we are not acting in love, we are in sin and outside of God's Divine covering. We are to quickly forgive and get under God's protection before satan attacks our bodies. Faith can only work by our love walk. Wisdom is to keep stating God's Word, instead of stating symptoms!

One who walks in the flesh realm cannot forgive his offenders. Walking in the Spirit and having God's grace operating through us enables us to forgive our offender. "God resists the proud, but gives grace to the humble" (Jas. 4:6).

Humility is a key to forgiveness! Humility helps us forgive and deal with hurt feelings. Otherwise, pride may make us take on the sin of unforgiveness. Hurt feelings, disappointments, and offenses are all big tools that satan uses to destroy us.

Life Is a Spiritual Battle

"For we do not wrestle against flesh and blood, but against principalities, against powers, against the rulers of the darkness of this age, against spiritual hosts of wickedness in the heavenly places" (Eph. 6:12).

Life is a spiritual battle. We are not fighting a flesh and blood battle with people. So do not get angry with the one that hurt you. Get angry with satan; resist him and he will flee. God's Word works if we keep our faith; stay out of sin, doubt, fear, and anger; and walk in love toward God and man.

We Can Have Assurance

"Assuredly, I say to you, whatever you bind on earth will be bound in Heaven, and whatever you loose on earth will be loosed in Heaven" (Matt. 18:18). That means that we must loose our offenders by not holding anger against them. Let God deal with them. We must forgive unconditionally, because God wants our hearts conformed to His pure love nature.

God's Way of Forgiveness

Psalms 103:12, "As far as the east is from the west, so far has He removed our transgressions from us." God set an example how we are to forgive. Jeremiah 31:34b says, "I will forgive their iniquity, and their sin I will remember no more." When we are in total forgiveness we no longer dwell upon the inflicted offense!

In Micah 7:19 we are told that God will cast all our sins into the depths of the sea. Once God forgives something, He buries it and never brings it up again. If we truly forgive, we do not bring it up again! The Word says, "And be kind to one another, tenderhearted, forgiving one another, even as God in Christ forgave you" (Eph. 4:32). So must we forgive!

It takes God's grace working through our lives to enable us to walk a love and forgiveness walk with offenders. James 4:6 says, God "gives grace to the humble." If we humble ourselves God's way, He will give us grace to forgive all offenders. Amen!

Be Alert to Satan's Plan

Satan suggests, entices and gets us then to reason, and then, he may stop us from forgiving someone by influencing our reasoning. He suggests that we do not have to forgive, because we were the one who was mistreated. That is his deceptive plan!

Jesus forgave, so we must forgive also. Never listen to satan. Instead, obey James 4:7-8, "Therefore, submit to God. Resist the devil and he will flee from you." Submitting to God is totally obeying His Word. John 1:1 proves that God and His Word are the same, so thereby, obeying the Word is obeying God. To trust God's Word is to trust God! Trusting God and resisting the symptom can stop defeat and give you victory!

Faith Requires Total Obedience

Faith connects us to God, as Hebrews 11:6a says, "Without faith it is impossible to please Him." Faith motivates, inspires, and helps us obey God's Word. True faith acts as if it is already done! "Abraham believed God, and it was accounted to him for righteousness" (Rom. 4:3). By faith, he obeyed and began offering up Isaac to God as his act of obedience. We may also have an obedience test sometime in life. But that test proves to be for our good, if we surrender and obey God's voice.

Abraham's heart was willing to sacrifice Isaac to God. Then God gave Isaac back to Abraham. When our hearts become willing to sacrifice everything to God in order to follow Him, He will then restore, and reward us more than we could ever imagine.

We Must Give Our All to God

I have given my all to follow God, as He requires first place. I have found that the rewards and benefits that He has given me in exchange for my life and my puny possessions are incomparable. I exchanged my sick body for abundant health, and the sickness and turmoil in my soul, for His peace in my mind!

Jesus Became Poor So We Could Inherit His Wealth

God gave Heaven's wealth in exchange for poverty, and joy and peace in exchange for sorrows. He gave me abundant life in exchange for death—He truly gave me a great exchange. Today I serve Him willingly with joy and gladness, because this is my reasonable sacrifice for His merciful, loving services!

My victory never came until I learned to use the Word of God as my Sword of the Spirit forcefully on satan. Then satan watched to see if I would be steadfast with my confessions. I convinced him that I believed God's Word was true by forcefully using chapter and verse on him. By using God's Word daily, I convinced satan I knew the authority that God's Word carries!

Satan watches to see if we will waver or doubt God's Word. We must stay steadfast, immovable, and faithful in our minds and in confessing God's promises. We can never show satan any sign of weakening faith. If we do, he will detect it and then try us even more. Battles are definitely fought within the mind. We settle the issue of life or death within our minds; then either healing or death, results from that decision! Amen!

Victory Is Based Upon Our Strong Expectation

Victory is based solely upon a strong expectation. Victory proves our faith was productive. We only know how strong our faith is when we get tried. We can win our battle by using God's Word just as Jesus did. Victory comes by faithfully enforcing the Word! I have intentionally repeated Scriptures often, as faith grows by hearing the Word repeated. (See Romans 10:17.)

Satan Hates the Day We Find God's Word and Use It

Satan is not afraid of my words unless they are God's Words that I say. I cannot yell loud enough with my own ability to scare him away. But oh how he hated the day I found God's Word and used it on him! In John 1:1, Jesus is the Word; He whipped satan! Now we have authority to use His Name. (See John 14:13.)

Jesus used the Word on satan when He was tempted in the wilderness. In Matthew 4:4 Jesus said, "It is written, man shall not live by bread alone, but by every word that proceeds from the mouth of God." If we obey that verse as Jesus did we also can drive the devil away for a season.

We Must Enforce the Word of God's Law

Jesus enforced God's law on satan as He used the Word on him; we must follow His example and put satan out! Law is no good unless enforced! God's Word is God's law, and it made satan back off from Jesus for a season when He used God's Word on him.

The Word of God is the Sword of the Spirit that defeated satan. He fears the Word since he was defeated by Jesus—who was the Word and then became the flesh man Jesus, according to John 1:10 and 14. Never fear; satan is a defeated foe!

Jesus battled and whipped satan and gave us authority and power to overcome him. (Luke 10:19; see also Colossians 2:15.)

In Matthew 16:18, Jesus said, ". . . the gates of hell shall not prevail against the Church." Know this, Jesus does not lie!

Within our body we are God's churches! Never allow satan's gates of hell to prevail against you—especially since Jesus defeated satan, and delegated us power to tread on him. It is my fault if I don't use my authority, or if I let satan defeat me!

Only lazy spirited people allow the enemy to defeat them after they have learned the truth! I know that statement may shake someone, and that is what I intended for it to do. Learn the power and authority that God's Word carries, and then forcefully execute the Word on satan. He will flee! Get violent now, and drive the enemy out. Then you can leave that defeated attitude behind, and gain your victory today!

Chapter 13

Diet Basics and the Healing Connection

God's Word has much to say about our diet. In Leviticus 11, God dedicated a full chapter to diet. Why do some think that we should not speak about the foods that we are feeding our bodies? In Genesis chapter 2, God said that Adam and Eve should not eat of the forbidden fruit. (See Genesis 2:17.) This was the first instance where God spoke about what man should not eat.

Psalms 139:14 says we are fearfully and wonderfully made. Our Father God made our bodies as a great masterpiece. Although He did this, our bodies cannot function properly for long without the right health care. God gave this responsibility to us! Most people take better care of their car than they do their body!

Spirit, Soul, and Body

God is a trinity. He is God our Father, God the Son, and God the Holy Spirit. We are a triune being made in God's image. We are a spirit, we have a soul, and we live in a body. Our spirit, soul, and body must harmonize together to function properly.

As God sees us through Jesus' Blood, He sees our spirit as perfected, though our flesh is not. Our flesh still wars with our spirit. We must submit our mind to agree with God's Word if our spirit is to function and cooperate with His laws.

Our body is the temple sheltering the Holy Spirit, who lives within us. (See 1 Corinthians 6:19.) We must be cautious of what we feed our bodies and choose good nutritious foods. I began a search for information to learn a new way to eat and how to properly care for my body. First I learned not to eat junk foods. Since then, my practices have paid off with good health.

I learned to supplement my diet with vitamins and minerals because of polluted air, water, soil, and food preservatives. Diets with preservatives and stale foods cannot build good cells. Cancer cells reproduce quickly on junk food diets.

We must choose wisely and read the labels on foods that we purchase. If we cannot define the word, then we must not eat it. Preservatives in our foods are harmful! If possible, we must prepare our own food. Only in the case of an emergency should we eat food from a tin container.

If filtered or spring water is available, don't drink chlorinated water. Chlorinated water isn't so good for us if it's used often. Our body handles filtered water much better.

Then we must feed our spirit on God's Word and meditate on it daily, as well as feeding our physical body; then feed our mind on God's goodness. If we are serious, God can show us how to feed our body so that we function properly. If we lack wisdom, let us ask of God, He gives it to us liberally (see Jas. 1:5).

We should live in an attitude of prayer, praise, and thanksgiving toward God. Our health will build up when we are cheerful. We must be thankful and always pray over all foods that we eat. We can hinder satan's health attacks by obeying all of God's commandments and laws, especially God's diet laws.

We must take care of our physical body as well as we care for our spirit-man. So many Christians are very sickly people. Satan has deceived them on what they eat. They think it doesn't matter because Jesus paid their sin debt, and so they think it's not important how they treat their body with improper foods.

God assigned us caretakers for our bodies. There-fore we need to be serious with all foods we put into them. Let's respect God's Spirit within by not eating preservative poisoned food.

In Genesis 3:17-18, God cursed the ground because Adam and Eve had sinned. He told them to eat herbs of the field. Herbs are healing. Some foods have little nutritional value. Supplements assist our diets that are deficient in many vitamins and minerals because of the stale dead foods that we eat.

In Leviticus chapter 11, God gave instructions about meats that we should and should not eat. He knew some animals' meat was not good for our bodies. He knew what was best for us as He made our bodies. You may ask if I eat meat. Yes, but I choose wisely!

Our bodies start decaying from the time of birth and continue to do so until the actual moment of death. Our goal must be to eat foods that delay the death process and build good cells. If we are good caretakers of our bodies, we will live longer and feel better while we are alive. In addition to our diet, God has given us certain laws that will help us to live longer. He said if we obey His laws, He will take sickness away from our midst. (See Exodus 15:26.) Obedience brings victory!

Here is an example of how a broken law can affect us. If we break the law of love, it throws our body out of kilter. For instance, if we get mad at someone and we do not forgive that person, we are not hurting that person as much as we are hurting ourselves. And if we hold unforgiveness in our hearts, we can pray but God will not hear or answer that prayer.

"If I regard iniquity in my heart, the Lord will not hear" (Ps. 66:18). Scientists have proven that when we hold anger within us, that anger causes our body to malfunction. Many illnesses have been reported when people do not obey God's forgiveness law, as faith works by love. (See Galatians 5:6.) I am convinced that without love, faith never works!

If we are serious with God, He will show us how to eat and stay healthy so that our bodies can function properly. We are a spirit, with a mind, will, and emotions, inside a body. We must never neglect any one part of our triune being that God made, or else our health will suffer and we will pay for that neglect.

If satan makes us think that we should only obey the Ten Commandments without proper nutrition, then he has deceived us. If we have believed that lie, it means that satan has won the battle over the appetite of our flesh, not our spirit. So never allow satan to fool you, as he fooled Eve through her appetite.

Deception is the name of satan's plan. I stress the importance of taking charge of our mind by feeding on the Word. Also, we need to supplement our diet and feed our body properly with good food, vitamins, minerals, herbs and enzymes.

When we do the best we can for ourselves, then God takes over and does what we cannot do for ourselves.

He does the impossible. He truly blesses and protects us if we do our best.

Junk Food Caution

Our bodies are products of foods that we eat, just as our minds are products of information that we feed and store inside them. We must not let satan deceive us by believing that we can function properly on junk foods. Satan deceived Eve with some fruit, so he can certainly deceive us if we allow him to.

When we feed our minds on God's Word and feed our bodies correctly, we can be assured God will reward us with our long life promise, as He said in Psalms 91:16, "With long life I will satisfy him." However, many die before their time from heart attacks, cancer, or some other disease caused by improper health care, junk foods, overeating, or by a big spirit of gluttony!

James 4:17, "To him who knows to do good and does not do it, to him it is sin." God said that if we obey His commandments, He would take sickness away from us. (See Exodus 15:26.)

When I was diagnosed with lupus in 1979, I was told that it was incurable. At one point I was given approximately 24 hours to live because my liver had completely stopped functioning. Another time my kidneys failed on a Friday night. This kidney failure lasted for more than 24 hours before I received help from God.

The next morning the Spirit of God told me to get someone to agree with me and stand upon Matthew 18:19 which says, "If two of you agree on earth concerning anything that they ask, it will be done..." I quickly obeyed God's instruction.

Although I was in critical condition at that moment, I obeyed, and God restored my kidneys to normal within two hours. He sent His Word and healed me just as Psalms 107:20 said He would. I have been healed since 1984. I strive to eat right, as staying well is worth my effort. I never want to be sick again!

It pays to obey God by heeding His Spiritual laws, taking care of our bodies, and eating correctly. Since I obeyed, I'm no longer sick or frail. Changing my diet worked! I feel wonderful at age 70. In 1970 I was aware that I needed to seek God's will concerning my health problems. I had realized nine years before my lupus diagnosis that no doctor could cure my health problems. I knew that my answer must come from God.

When my doctor diagnosed me with lupus, he told me lupus was incurable. Back in 1970 I learned that if I would study God's Word, eat nutritious foods, and use Scripture, nothing would be incurable with God. So I practiced good nutrition and I used God's Word. They both rewarded me well, praise the Lord!

When I became interested in nutrition, I sought out ways to take better care of my body and my spirit. I spent much time listening to famous lecturers who were teaching on nutrition. I bought books and tapes that taught me how diet, lifestyle, and environment can break down our body's defenses. I stayed in God's Word daily and fed my spirit as well. My study paid off. I found that my diet would help me get well if it was corrected.

A faulty diet and bad environment lowers the immune system and brings down my resistance that God designed to help me overcome disease. If I correct my diet, my body heals. God placed within my body an ability to heal itself if I have proper nutrition. If I cut my finger and my body is healthy, my finger heals quickly. But, if my body is short of nutrition, my finger heals slowly. If healing comes slowly, that may indicate that I have not taken care of my body with proper nutrition, or I may have failed to drink plenty of pure water.

There are children who inherited disease-related illnesses due to inadequate nutritional intake by the mother before their birth. That was my case. My mother never properly ate or got medical help before I was born. God never held me accountable for her failure, though I suffered from deficiency.

I am grateful that I discovered how to care for my body nutritionally and also learned to apply healing Scriptures to my health problem. Combining nutrition with God's Word paid off. Since 1984, my healing example has helped many sick ones. I'm an example that anyone's health can return after a bad diagnosis, by eating nutritiously and executing healing Scriptures!

God is sovereign. If He chooses to instantly heal us, then He will. That is His healing gift in operation, and God's Word says in First Corinthians 12:11, it is as the Spirit Himself wills! God has instantly healed me twice. However, with lupus it was not instant, so I began to study how to help myself. What God showed me will help you as well. He showed me that I was a three-part being and that I must obey the following steps:

1. Guard my spirit and obey His laws of love and forgiveness.

2. Feed my soul (mind, will, and emotions) on His Word.

3. Care for my body to the best of my ability.

By taking authority over my mind, feeding my spirit on God's Word, and changing my diet, I saw amazing results. I also read in Proverbs 18:21, "Death and life are in the power of the tongue." So I spoke life into my body to put my faith in motion. God's Word says faith without works, or action, is dead. I called things that were not as though they were. (See Romans 4:17.) I wanted my body well, so I called my body healthy and strong, as that is God's method of changing unwanted conditions.

It would be sin for me to abuse my body by eating junk food since I have learned how to eat properly. (See James 4:17.) If foods we eat don't build good cells, then our improper food breaks down destroying existing ones. We should question whether the foods we eat build or tear down, thereby lowering the immune system.

If we stop and think before stuffing things in our mouth, we will be less likely to indulge. This rule applies to food or medicines. An exception may be that one has an emergency situation and a medicine is vital for health or to save his life. Otherwise, we should follow God's good nutrition laws.

I stay well by my obedience to God's laws. I take no medicine and I have no need to. I have no pain or sickness. I was once on loads of medication. Now I am free from them all. The only pills that I now take are vitamins, minerals, digestive enzymes, and balanced herbal formulas that help to build good health.

God speaks of herbs in the Bible, so I follow a wonderful herbal plan. I eat right, confess right words, worship God, and read His Word. I desire to stay well and strong because satan attacks people who neglect their health and keep weak bodies.

God will help all those in need when they worship and delight themselves in Him. "Delight yourself also in the Lord, and He shall give you the desires of your heart" (Ps. 37:4). "No good thing will He withhold from those who walk uprightly" (Ps. 84:11). I wanted good health so I could serve God better. Healing came as I changed old neglectful health habits!

We all need to pray and seek God for better ways to care for ourselves. It is important to stay out of worry, as our frame of mind can affect our health and can stop our faith from trusting God's promises. Worried minds cannot hold strong faith!

If I abuse or poison myself, I cannot expect God to keep healing me over and over again. God has given me a second chance. I try to stay disciplined, eat right, keep my thoughts right, and say right words. I now have faith to believe that God can keep me well, as I am obeying these principles.

I know God's laws are perfect and good. He wants us well. If you believe God and obey His laws, He will help you just as He has helped me. God is no respecter of persons.

Healing Requires Total Forgiveness

Instructions on forgiveness are found in Ephesians 4:32. Forgiveness means always walking in love. We must not hang onto old hurts, but release and let all hurts go. God can heal scars, as He came into the world to heal the brokenhearted. (See Luke 4:18.) Let Him heal your broken heart now! You can get your body healed if you eat properly and forgive your offenders. God has given us so many blessing promises. Following are some of them.

God's Precious Promises

Psalms 118:17, "I shall not die, but live." Also, "With long life I will satisfy him" (Ps. 91:16). "Call to Me, and I will answer you" (Jer. 33:3a). Oh, what promises; let's claim them!

God Is Love and Satan Is Evil!

God proved His love unconditionally at Calvary. Isaiah 53:1 says, "Who has believed our report?" If we don't believe His report, it's because we have failed to fellowship with God.

By my own experiences, I know God's promises are true. But they are conditional. We must obey His instructions, such as things like nutritional laws, reading His Word, and obeying His love law. Satan makes us prove our faith by putting our faith on trial. He surely made me prove my faith! But as our faith is tried our soul gets purified. The trying of faith is necessary.

Our faith must stay strong while at the same time we strive to eat right. If we don't eat properly, we cannot gain strength for the faith battle. God expects us to take good care of our bodies. Then He helps us stay well, if we stay in right relationship with God and in fellowship with people also.

Although Jesus' mission was to heal and restore, that fact alone does not excuse our responsibility to obey His health law. If I eat dead food my body cannot build. It will die. If I eat living food my body can revive and live. Food is alive when first harvested. Food that lies for weeks is dead. So enzymes, vitamins, and minerals that were once there are now depleted.

Overcooking destroys valuable enzymes and minerals that our food contained when it was harvested. High heat also destroys nutritional content. Steam vegetables on low heat for no more than five or ten minutes; then remove from the heat and eat immediately. Never cook food submersed in water, as valuable nutrition is lost to the water.

Steamed vegetables must be eaten as near raw as possible if one desires to rebuild his health. Use stainless steel cookware for cooking if possible. Juicing vegetables builds health also.

We must seek ways to take better care of our bodies. If we stay in faith we will get God's attention. Then we gain His favor, especially when He knows we are seriously obeying His health laws and stating His Word over satan's attack as well! When I got serious I was blessed more than I ever expected.

I have proven that God's Word works if I obey His health laws and use His Word for my spirit battle. God honors and rewards honest efforts, just as He rewards those seeking wisdom on how to better care for themselves. His reward is good health.

Victory comes by using God's Word, eating right, and controlling my mind. There is nothing too hard for God. If you follow the steps I have written you can climb out of your health problems. God will help you if you will be hopeful and help yourself. Then be willing to help others! God heals today by many avenues. Take His promises seriously by firmly standing upon them. Practice good nutritional habits and follow God's laws. "Man shall not live by bread alone, but by every Word of God!" (Luke 4:4) We live by God's Word, plus nutrition!

Chapter 14

Healing Testimonials

One day while I was working as a United Parcel Service delivery driver, I fell and slipped a disc in my back. I called my supervisor and told him that I had injured my back. He came quickly to ride with me while I stood driving my truck, because he did not know the route. I could barely move and was in great pain, so he lifted the packages that we delivered.

Emily Dotson had a package for delivery that day. I had met her many times while delivering packages to her home. When she saw someone else delivering, she asked about me. My supervisor told her I was in my truck with a bad back. Emily came to my truck and said she could help me. I had no idea what she meant.

She told me to come down from my truck so she could pray for me.

I almost fell while getting out because I was in so much pain. Emily kept me from falling, while her husband ran and got a straight-back chair for me to sit in beside the truck. My supervisor and I looked at each other, wondering what was going on. Emily's husband lifted my feet straight out, telling me to notice that one leg was two inches shorter than the other.

Emily prayed, asking God to move and align my spine. Then as my eyes were closed and I listened, I felt my back begin to loosen as my discs moved. I looked at my feet and they were the same length once again. I felt no pain, but was afraid to move because I never wanted to hurt again. Emily told me to get up, bend, stoop, and do anything I wanted. I slowly stood and bent over, moved, and stepped into my truck. I had no pain at all. I could hardly believe what had happened. As I thanked Emily, my supervisor stood speechless. He even told his church about it on Sunday.

I still visit Emily whenever I can. She has helped me since then with other pains and problems, and I thank God for directing me to Emily that day. She is so sweet and caring. She is a very special person. Love, Colleen H. Smith, July 1998.

I am writing about my granddaughter, Kassandra Kay Neal. She was born in Eugene, Oregon, April 30,

1986, with a deformity in both hip sockets. When she began to walk she was pigeon-toed and in constant pain. Pain caused her to cry herself to sleep nightly or to awaken in the night crying in pain. She would need medication to get back to sleep.

Medical doctors advised her mother, my daughter, to allow Kassandra to have corrective surgery on her hip sockets but my daughter didn't have the money. So she moved, bringing Kassandra from Oregon to Illinois in July 1990, when Kassandra was age four. They did this to be near her Grandpa and Grandma, the Rev. and Mrs. Joseph Cusic, pastors of "Church on the Way" in Alton, Illinois.

In October 1990, Evangelist Emily Dotson came to Alton to hold a healing service at our church. I encouraged my daughter to take Kassandra to the meeting that night. When Evangelist Dotson prayed for Kassandra, the power of God went through her deformed hip sockets. She was completely healed in one instant by the power of Jesus that night.

God healed Kassandra so well that now, at 13, she is taking ice skating lessons. She is also active in gymnastics. She remains healed since 1990, through 1999, and she is in no pain at all. Praise God! Sincerely, Patty Cusic, Kassandra's grandmother, January 24, 1999.

Emily, we still praise the Lord for your ministry, and for your being used by God to help Sheryl! We received the tape set from the healing seminar you taught in April at Dr. Norvel Hayes's ministry, and have again been blessed by your diligent Word-filled teaching. We pray for the Lord's blessing on your life and ministry and especially for your strength.

All healing power comes from God and from His anointing, and true ministers of God are called by Him and anointed for His service. It is not you, but His Spirit in you, doing the work. But that high calling requires dedication, perseverance, patience, love, and all other works of a mature Christian. That does not come without a price. And satan does not find any joy in your ministry. I know he puts up a fight! Your dedication and hard work truly give God a vessel so usable for His service.

As we praise and worship God for your blessed anointing, we lift you up as His servant and praise God for you! As I listened to your tape set, I was struck with a distinct impression that I need to explain.

First, I have served in some capacity with the Navy and Marine Corps for 27 years, my entire working life. So I tend to see things from that point of view. Second, and I say this as the highest compliment, in listening to you I heard the voice of the Combat Strict Drill Sergeant preparing His recruits for battle.

War is the embodiment of hell in our world, as chaos and insanity run rampant. The good soldier must learn to make some sense and survive. A great soldier does that and goes forward, takes ground, defeats the enemy, and wins the battle. I think General Patton said (in courser terms), "Our duty is not to die for our country, but to make the other man die for his country."

Christians involved in spiritual warfare are in a place that Marines call the "cutting edge of the sword." We are at war; a particularly dirty war of the worst sort. The enemy is attacking our homes, and our children are his favorite targets!

Emily, you are a great soldier in God's army. I thank you for imparting your hard-won combat experience to us so that we may join the fight and carry the battle forward! I am certain you receive criticism for your absolute devotion and unending dedication to the Word of God, but that is from those who don't know about war or warfare. So never give in! God bless you, Emily, and please let us know your future schedule. Sincerely, Greg and Sheryl Jones, 1996.

Thank you, Emily, for the two tapes you sent me. They are excellent. One tape was "Dr. Norvel Hayes Interviews Emily Dotson." The other tape was Emily teaching, "The Cost of Deception." If someone really wants to be healed, those two tapes have all the information they would need. I have enjoyed hearing the tapes very much. I really praise God for you, Emily, and for Dr. Norvel Hayes.

I praise God for your obedience to make those tapes available for people like me and for others all

over America. Through those tapes many may find
God and find healing. Emily, I am glad to have met
you personally. I always tell people about you. I thank
you for praying for me and helping me with all that
you have. God bless you as you continue to work for
Him! Your brother in Christ, Buddy Tate, 1996.

As a 12-year-old in 1977, I battled with stomach
cancer and had survived after having stomach surgery, radiation, and chemotherapy. In March 1989,
leiomayosarcoma had returned in all three lobes of my
liver as well as my gallbladder. I was given radiation
and chemotherapy. I was given only six to twelve
weeks to live. Although my doctor offered me
chemotherapy, it was experimental and he did not expect me to survive. My husband, Mike, knew that our
God is a God of His Word. If God has said that I was
healed by the stripes of Jesus, then he believed that I
was healed.

Though I knew that God could heal people, I was
not sure that He would bother to heal me. I decided to
take chemotherapy just in case God wouldn't heal me.
Mike and I argued over this for a number of weeks. He
knew I could not live by his faith, so he prayed for God
to show me that it was His will to heal me.

Mike called Emily after he read her testimony of
healing from lupus in Norvel Hayes's newsletter. After
Emily told us how God had healed her through Jesus

Christ, she prayed for me and then encouraged us to come to Norvel Hayes's upcoming meeting.

I learned that God made provision through Jesus, and that He is no respecter of persons. Then I received faith for healing of terminal liver cancer on July 6, 1989, and chose not to take chemotherapy. Although I had expected instant physical healing, it came gradually. Though my commitment to Jesus was strengthened continually in my daily prayer time, my weakness, tumors, and cancer symptoms did not leave immediately.

A CT scan in July 1989 revealed that the tumors had stabilized. They were neither growing nor shrinking. But I began growing in my personal relationship with Jesus. I committed myself to the work of God through a stable church, and was encouraged by Christians like Emily, who understand the power of God's Word. The activity and encouragement helped keep me strong in my faith.

Though I still had symptoms of fatigue, the malabsorption and pain gradually disappeared from my body within six months. We wanted a baby very much, so I called Emily and she prayed that we would have a baby. After that, I became pregnant with my first child, though I had been told that I was sterile. Against my doctor's advice, I carried her to full term. Two years later I gave birth to a healthy baby boy.

After his birth in 1993, I had another CT scan. The results were rather perplexing for the team of doctors involved. Although the scan revealed tumors on my liver, the test revealed the tumors were all dead! My doctor will not tell me that I am healed of liver cancer, although I know the same Spirit that raised Christ Jesus from the dead dwells in me and has quickened or given life to my mortal body. (See Romans 8:11.) Jeanne Marie Wrobel, Buffalo, New York, July 1999.

My wife, two daughters, and I attended a church service at Asheboro Christian Center where Emily ministered. Our seven-year-old daughter, Jessalyn, had been suffering from asthma attacks for several weeks. Her asthma medication cost about $200 per month. She went down for prayer at the end of the service. Emily prayed for Jessalyn and called her healed.

She accepted her healing by faith that night. After prayer she refused her medication. She has had no symptoms of asthma since then. Emily also prayed for our four-year-old daughter, Rachel, and her boldness for the Lord increased. My wife, Lisa, and I also accepted the call to preach the gospel that night. Thanks, Emily, for your prayers. The Jones family: Jim, Lisa, Jessalyn and Rachel, March 1996.

On the following pages are miracles that I, Emily Dotson, have witnessed and recall happening after I had taught healing classes, and then began my prayer service at various churches.

One night I ministered in Brady, Texas, and a man paralyzed on his left side was brought up for prayer. As I prayed, the power of God went through him and completely healed him. No one informed me that the man could not speak a word. After I prayed for him I said, "Sir, God gave you a miracle. Repeat after me and thank the Lord for healing you." Praise God, he clearly repeated each word that I told him to say!

Later that night I found that before prayer he had been unable to speak. God healed his brain, restored his speech, and restored full strength to his left side. The church was overjoyed. I praise God and give Him all the glory!

Once as I ministered in Cleveland, Tennessee, at Dr. Norvel Hayes's church, a lady came up for prayer. Though she had already had three mouth surgeries, she needed one more. She said it was so painful that she did not want to have it, but wanted to trust God. I looked in her mouth and saw a large opening where surgery was needed to close a hole where a tooth had been extracted.

I prayed for her, then she started to return to her seat. As she took a few steps she jumped up and down shouting, "A tooth, a tooth!" I said, "Come back." Then I looked in her mouth and discovered that God had filled in the empty hole with a big, white new tooth. Praise God! I got excited with her, and the entire audience began shouting together with us that day.

Again as I taught healing classes in Brady, Texas, God gave sight to three blind people who already had had unsuccessful surgical implants. I tested them. They could not see daylight. After prayer, all had perfect vision. I praise God for healing them!

Once I ministered in Wilson, North Carolina. After I had spoken that night, a lady came into my prayer line. She was 45 years old and had been born with a deformed hip socket. She later told me that one leg had always been two inches shorter that the other leg. God healed her completely as I laid hands on her hip before I even had time to pray.

As quickly as my hands touched her, I felt the awesome movement of the Holy Spirit bumping my hands up and down, molding her hip socket. We both got excited and began to praise God. Then she told me about the short leg. Now she had two legs the same length. She said that as she heard me teach, she knew God would heal her. God met her expectation!

Two years ago, I taught healing classes at a church in Woodstown, New Jersey. A lady came with great pain with lupus. She had knots on her neck and could scarcely walk down the church aisle. That Sunday after I taught and was praying for people in the prayer line, I suddenly heard her shout as she sat on the front row. I looked at what was happening. She was shouting, jumping, and leaping under God's anointed power. And her knots had vanished!

God completely healed her as she sat on the pew. She ran all over the church totally pain free. She received her miracle. She did not leave church the way she came, in Jesus' Name!

Jesus is the same yesterday, today, and tomorrow, but man limits His power. God only operates where faith is present. I have found that teaching God's Word brings the anointing for miracles to operate in the services. Then His power manifests.

One thing I have noticed, as I minister, is that people who do not have a personal relationship with the Lord will come to church looking to me for their healing. I tell them that I cannot heal a flea, yet I feel their spirits pulling on me. Everyone must know that Jesus is the Healer. I can disappoint them, but Jesus cannot. People must get acquainted with Jesus by reading their Bible, praying, worshiping, and praising God.

If people want a miracle, they must create an atmosphere and an environment that God will come into. God never comes to an atmosphere where there is doubt, confusion, strife, or anger. He performs miracles where peace and expectant faith abide.

When I minister, I like to teach two sessions before I pray for the people. God's Word must increase their faith, and then they are ready to receive healing. Jesus is always ready to give, but people are not always ready to receive. They need to be taught how to receive from God by having expectant faith.

If one comes for prayer to be healed before understanding how to receive, he gets frustrated and leaves disappointed when he is not healed. He must be prepared to receive from God. We must teach them to receive healing. How can we receive gold if it rains down and our basket is upside down? God continuously pours out His anointing and miracles, but we must be expecting and reaching in faith to receive them from Him!

When people are taught correctly, they will receive every time, as God is watching and ready to give according to the faith expectation level. Dr. Oral Roberts is famous for saying, "Expect a miracle." If we never expect one, we never receive from God. We have to believe Him to receive from His hand!

Hebrews 11:6 warns us that we cannot please God unless we believe that He will reward us for believing, and diligently seeking Him. So seek God, don't just seek His handout! If we diligently seek God He can fill all emotional and physical need!

Healing comes from God to our souls, and then goes out through our bodies. Illness from satan likewise goes to the soul, then to the body. Just as a healthy tree root gives sap to make a tree healthy, so does our mind control our health. If our souls and our minds prosper, then our health prospers as well.

We do not come in the world knowing it all. We must be taught. If you have a lazy spirit, do not expect to receive a miracle from God. Miracles come from God when you are hungry and eagerly expecting them. God seldom gives great miracles to lazy people. We must strive not to be lazy!

God's mercies and compassions do not fail; they are new every morning, and His faithfulness is great. (See Lamentations 3:22-23.) God is faithful; He rewards us for seeking after Him. God is not just a "give me, give me God." We need to give Him our time, talents, and worship. God knows if we are serious.

God wrote 66 books of letters in the Bible. Have you read them? He is the only Physician who can heal the body and soul. We can find Him if we seek Him with our whole heart. When we find Him, we will not have to seek an earthly physician. Jesus is the same Physician now as He was when He walked on earth. So reach by faith and take a miracle from God! Amen!

Chapter 15

Active Faith Produces Results

Here are some qualities found in faith's operation: hope, trust, patience, love, joy, and obedience.

Hope is faith's starter. Godly hope boosts, inspires, and guides, adding strength to help faith reach its goal. Hope is in future-tomorrow zone. Tomorrow's hope is not productive without faith, and cannot yield tangible results. A time must be established so that hope can turn into "now faith" or future-faith is not productive. Yesterday's hope is always trailing now-faith. The hope rocket has boosted, doing its job. So "now-faith" takes over, completing the task.

Trust comes by knowing God on a one-to-one basis, by personally spending time with Him in relationship.

Trusting God never comes by casual acquaintance. Without a relationship, God remains a stranger so that we cannot trust Him. Through intimacy with God we become certain that He can and He will do all His Word says. In our intimacy we trust and rest with confidence.

Faith trusts that God is able, credible, and willing to keep us well. Faith knows that God never allows harm to destroy us. Without intimacy we cannot trust that God will heal us from any deadly attack. Hope and trust are like Siamese twins. They cannot be separated as our patience-glue connects them together. Our patience-glue bonds to faith and never lets faith go!

Patience is a strong ingredient that we find in faith's operation. Patience is faith's strengthening quality; it buys our needed time for faith to produce without aborting the faith-seed before maturity. Luke 8:15 says fruit comes with patience. Hebrews 6:12 says through faith and patience we inherit the promises. Patience is a quality of God's character that we need more of, as it creates a no-quitting determination!

Consider Job as the father of patience, just as Abraham was the father of faith. God gave Abraham a promise so he glued Job's patience to it, then received his promise. Patience added to faith hastens victory, sealing secure the promise!

Love is faith's vital ingredient. My faith works only if I walk by love, Galatians 5:6 says. In first Corinthians 13:13 we are told that love never fails. Love is the strongest force in the universe. We may have faith to move mountains, but if we don't have godly love, that faith cannot help us gain our promise.

Love is an ingredient that so many fail to add to faith. Then they wonder why their faith never produces. Forgiveness is acting by love enough to forgive the offender. By overlooking the faults of our offenders faith can then produce substance!

Joy germinates a faith seed, keeping it alive. Our faith seed matures quickly as we obey God's love law. Love can bond joy to a faith seed, securing patience for my faith seed's maturity. So keep a joyful attitude or you can cause faith's seed to abort before faith reaches its maturity. Joy is vital; the Word says, "The joy of the Lord is your strength" (Neh. 8:10).

Obedience always brings blessings. Not walking in love is disobedience and brings curses. (See 1 Samuel 1:15-22.) Unless I obey God's law of love and walk in forgiveness, faith for healing becomes unproductive. But there is another ingredient to add, called now-faith—it stays in a now realm, in present tense.

We never have God's kind of now-faith until it comes from God's Word. Other information gives non-productive future-faith, a false hoping-faith. Hoping-faith remains in tomorrow's future! Future-faith of tomorrow never produces, as tomorrow's faith never gives fruit. Our productive faith is now, this moment!

True faith never operates in carnal, non-spiritually minded people. They never walk in love, and they lack patience in understanding God's faith operation. Faith works by a love walk of God's character that is totally opposite of unforgiveness!

God calls faith as calling things that are not, as though they are already complete. Things that God calls appear! Faith creates them, making them exist. His method works for us, whether it is health or wealth! God's method is found in Mark chapter 11. We have our desires by believing without doubting and by saying it; then we can have our desires met by God! (See Mark 11:23.)

However, certain conditions must be met before our confessions can produce. Confessing the Word while being full of unforgiveness will not work. Never expect God to give what you desire if you are in sin! Sin stops up our channel to God by stopping the flow of His blessings from coming down upon us.

We must combine hope, trust, patience, love, joy, and obedience to our faith as we wait for a healing manifestation. Then our spirit can rest. God's promises will produce peace, if we trust His Word and patiently wait and quote His promises. God rewards obedience when He sees that we strongly trust His Word. Hebrews 11:6 proves that by trusting God, He rewards us. Patience and faith settle our doubting issues.

Romans 12:3 says that God has dealt to every man the measure of faith. Our faith weakens if it's not connected with patience and trust. If faith weakens, we may commit the sin of doubting. "Whatever is not of faith is sin" (Rom. 14:23). By fellowshipping with God and spending quality time with Him, our faith and trust bond and grow stronger. Then we don't carry the sin of doubting God's credibility.

Our time spent fellowshipping with God and reading His Word is refreshing and rewarding. We gain faith for big blessings that a disobedient one never can. Intimacy drives fears out. Be cautious. Don't allow satan to rob your faith by a fear spirit, as that spirit creates doubts that stops faith's operation.

Hebrews chapter 11 tells of many of God's people who met faith's requirements to obtain their promises. No devil stopped their faith, as they all had the ingredients that I previously stated.

Our faith is vital as faith fills us with more life, but fear demands death. Fear means satan has robbed and may kill unless we keep the fear door shut and faith's switch on. Fear is a trap that satan uses to get us out from under our faith covering.

A fear spirit cancels faith for our power that Jesus delegated to us in Luke 10:19, and then we get defeated.

An Overcoming Confession

We need to confess and say, "Fear, leave me now in Jesus' Name. You cannot rob faith and trust from me. God keeps His promises. He cannot lie. Satan, you are a liar. You cannot make your fear spirit remain! I will not stay in your trap. Get out now! I say the fear spirit from hell must leave me now!"

Say, "Fear, I will not allow you to remain in me. The Spirit of Jesus lives in me and He is greater than fear. In Luke 10:19, Jesus delegated me power and authority over all the powers of my enemy. Therefore, your fear spirit will vacate, because I enforce my delegated power on this spirit in Jesus' Name. I say go and never return. My faith in God seals my heart's door shut to fear!" God cannot lie. (See Titus 1:2.) Say, "God gave me promises and He cannot lie. God makes all His promises sure."

Say loudly, "I confess that my faith is maturing. I am being as fully persuaded as Abraham was. I will trust God's report instead of a doctor's report. I disregard all other reports of lying symptoms! I believe God's Word gives me healing as I now believe that God's Word is His true report!"

My Poem: "Rest Inside Satan's Storm"

By reading this short poem, you can know Jesus never let me go.

Often I did say, "Jesus rides on the waves in
my storm today."
We must not fear as Jesus is near, so now to
you I can relay,

When the storm was ready to kill, Jesus said,
peace be still.
Then the storm settled down when Jesus spoke
His perfect will!

As illness strikes, stormy, wild emotions can be tamed and our emotions can be laid to rest, by combining hope, trust, patience, love, joy and faith. Within that strong combination, no storm is too big for Jesus to calm, He will say, "Peace be still." Storms lie down in peace, then they will cease!

"If you abide in Me, and my words abide in you, you will ask what you desire, and it shall be done for you" (John 15:7). This proves we overcome by abiding in God's Word, then faith gets God involved. So check your faith by God's standard:

1. Faith never observes encountered circumstances.
2. Faith enables us to walk above the circumstances.
3. Faith will never doubt, waver, or look backwards.
4. Faith always thinks and acts in a positive manner.
5. Faith stops the doubt issue by waiting on a promise.
6. Faith is not afraid of giants; faith attacks them.

7. Faith will motivate us to climb over the mountain.

8. Faith sees no impossibilities, but looks for answers.

9. Faith looks for victory and never thinks negatively.

10. Faith never gives up and does not know how to quit.

11. Faith never sees a doctor's report as the final one.

12. Faith knows God's Word is the final and true report.

13. Faith is fearless although danger lurks nearby.

14. Faith accepts First Peter 2:24 and will obey Mark 11:23.

15. Faith knows God's report overrides all other reports!

Faith anchors us in God's Word so no doctor's report can defeat us. "The just shall live by faith" (Heb. 10:38). Without strong faith, we never please God. To please God, we live by faith in God and His Word, and then disregard all symptoms!

Vital Information

If symptoms or negative reports can stop me from my faith confessions or cause me not to act on God's

Word, then satan has stolen the Word from my heart! Although the Word of God may still be in my head, that head knowledge doesn't produce unless I confess God's Word with my mouth. God's Word produces from my heart and opens my mouth to make a channeled pipeline to God.

Strong faith joyfully thanks God that by His Word we are healed—before we feel healed. That is living by faith and not by fleshly feelings. Feelings cannot alter God's Word, but God's Word can alter symptoms and change a bad report into a good report!

The promises that God swore to Abraham are rightfully ours. However they only become ours if we accept Jesus as Savior and believe the credibility of God's Word. Galatians 3:29 says God made us heirs to the promise. We inherited Abraham's blessings because Jesus freed us from satan's trap of sin and sickness.

When I needed healing, I searched God's Word and found promises of healing. Then I started my serious confessions. I was told that healing Scriptures could make me well if by faith I quoted them diligently. That was my only hope at the time, so I obeyed and the Word turned my life from defeat into victory!

I may have been spared much pain and could have been healed sooner if I had spoken the Word over mountainous problems earlier. But it's never too late to seek God. By speaking God's Word continually, my mind turned and agreed with God's Word!

Faith's Spiritual Battle Is Mental

Faith's spiritual battle is mental. The mind is a control center where information is stored to bring success or failure. As we fill our minds with God's Word we gain victory over satan. Read Ephesians 6:10-18 to learn how to win the battle over principalities, powers, and spiritual wickedness by using that Word. Then satan cannot gain access to our mind to use for a battleground, to inject thoughts that are contrary to the Word.

Faith is an ingredient that God calls just. Faith-filled words act as swords to battle the enemy so our victory can come!

We absolutely must speak God's Word or satan can defeat us!

By filling our mind with God's Word, satan has no room to inject his negative thoughts. As satan's negative words bombard our mind we must use God's Word to replace that turmoil with peace.

Document Your Statement

It is good to make a written statement of the day, month, and time that you cursed the lying symptoms and believed God for your healing. Below was my documented statement:

"Today, Friday, January 21, 1983, at 1:45 p.m., I accepted healing from lupus through faith in God's promise. By the stripes of Jesus I am healed according to First Peter 2:24, and by the Isaiah 53:5 report. I will never doubt God's Word again!

"I will not look back to yesterday. I call myself healed today and I will call myself healed tomorrow. I hold this date and document before you, Lord, and I also hold it before satan as a memorial forever! I call my healing as already done. I have now-faith that produces health and healing in my body! Amen!"

My declaration worked and it will work for you! I quoted that date daily without wavering. Many days satan sent pain and tormenting spirits to torture me. He tried to make me doubt, but I stayed steadfast with my confession despite the pain. My faith in God's Word gave me strong patience to wait for my healing manifestation. No devil could talk me out of faith once the truth of God's report settled inside my mind and my heart. I became fully persuaded that God's Word was true. My doctor's report could not override God's Word. My faith started to work and never stopped operating until its task was complete!

After my documentation, I spoke of lupus in the past tense. I never looked back. I rested from anxiety, worry, and fear, as I knew fear never came from God. I made a quality decision to be happy. As I rejoiced, my body was building good cells and my faith was working. The joy of the Lord gave me strength that enabled me to recover from both systemic and discoid lupus.

Faith's Declaration

Faith will say, "Get out satan, I believe Mark 11:23. My mountain of illness is coming down! It is moving now. I receive my healing that Jesus paid for. I say by Psalms 118:17 that I will live and not die, as I am abiding daily in Psalms 91."

Say, "I am receiving my healing according to the report of Isaiah 53:5. Satan, you cannot deceive me. I walk in faith and you cannot shake my mind. My faith in God's Word anchors my mind and my faith holds me safe, settled, and secure! I trust God's Word and I will rise above the storms that you send against my spirit, soul, and body. Peace and joy win my battle over you!"

As we confess the Word with faith's strong combination, we get God's favor and keep it. Praise God, my faith battle turned my defeat into victory by my confession of God's Word. God's method works if your faith remains strong. So anchor your faith on the Word, and you can leave defeat behind and go on to victory! Amen!

Chapter 16

My Last Big Accident

In April 1998, while I was in Tulsa, Oklahoma, at Rev. Dave Roberson's church seminar, I met a dear Christian by the name of Dorcas. She greeted me and related what a blessing my tape albums and small healing handbook, entitled "Miracle Healing Power," had been to her over the past five years. I told her that I was in the process of writing a larger book, but that the manuscript completion had slowed down. I did not have a computer so I was dependent on others for typing assistance.

Two days later, she told me that God had told her to buy me a computer. I was taken by surprise and said, "That surely was the Lord's voice." She said that she wanted part of the reward that God would give me for writing my book. I then related to her that I would gladly be willing to share my reward with her.

We hugged and praised God that she had heard the Holy Spirit and had obeyed Him. My heart was glad that I would have my own computer to get my book ready for printing. Now I could finish my book at home without depending upon others!

I came home after the meeting in Tulsa, looking forward to getting my new computer. The company she ordered it from had a delay in shipping the order, so I had to wait until the last of April before I received my gift. Finally, the day arrived and the computer came. Dorcas had purchased the whole works. She bought a computer, CD-ROM, scanner, and printer. What a blessing this gift was for me! At last I could type my book at home!

Before I started typing, I had to wait for my grandson who attends North Carolina State University to come home and assemble my computer. Although I was anxious to start, I had made reservations to go to a church conference about 115 miles away. I had no time to work before leaving for the conference. I would have to wait until I returned home to start typing my book.

The last week of April I left home to attend the meeting. Satan had heard all the plans, so he was getting ready to launch a big attack on me. I was unaware of his big plan, or of what he would do on the day those church services would end.

Some friends met me at the meeting, and we had a wonderful time together in the Lord. The church conference was wonderful, and the anointing of the Lord was great. I sang and danced before the Lord at those wonderful worship services, and I drank in all the wonderful anointing.

I danced before the Lord at all those great services. Can you believe that? That does not seem possible, does it? No way, considering that I was once paralyzed in bed and had doctors tell me that I would be an invalid the rest of my life. They never thought Jesus could heal my paralyzed back.

In those church services, I was filled with joy and drank in the wonderful anointing. Then on Sunday morning, May 3, 1998, the conference ended. I had planned to go home immediately to work on my book. However, an accident altered my plan. I did not get to go home until three days after the conference ended.

On that Sunday morning, May 3, I drove to the last church service. When I arrived, I parked across the street where construction work was being done because the church parking lot was already filled. My friend and I crossed the street to attend the final service before going home that day.

When crossing the street I noticed large gravel spilled on the parking lot. Construction trucks had spun a thick layer of large, jagged gravel out onto the cement-paved street from the parking lot we had crossed. As I looked down, I thought, "What a mess! I must be careful as that loose gravel could throw me down." Although I was careful, the loose gravel threw me like a roller skate and I fell swiftly onto the cement-paved street.

As I was falling, my mind raced, and I thought, "Not my head, satan!" I know that is what he had planned. Satan wanted my head to hit the sharp, jagged, graveled rock and kill me. Yet as I was falling I was able to stiffen my neck and keep my head from hitting the dangerous jagged rocks.

I was unable to break my swift fall because I carried my purse and Bible in one hand, and a tote bag with my dress heels in the other. This appeared to be a direct attack by satan. And I was unable to use my hands to break the swift, dangerous fall.

As I landed, I knew something was dreadfully wrong. I was unable to get up. The instant I fell, a car suddenly stopped beside me. Two occupants jumped out, one saying, "I am a doctor, and this is my wife." I thought, "Lord, you sure sent help quickly." My friend introduced me to them, and then the doctor said he had heard of me and was glad to meet me. Then he stooped down and shook my hand as I lay there on the street.

I looked up to Heaven stating, "Lord, I don't know why this happened, but eventually I shall know the reason." The doctor said, "I am reason number one." He exclaimed he wanted to meet me but was sorry that it had to be this way. He was attending the same church service, but we never would have met otherwise, because the church conference attendance was so large.

He said he felt sure my hip was broken as I could not get up. He called an ambulance and followed the ambulance to the hospital. He and his wife were truly sent by God. They stayed until the x-rays were taken, which showed I needed surgery. I was placed in a private room. There the doctor and his wife sent me beautiful flowers. They were truly a blessing to me!

There was no surgeon on duty at the small hospital where I was taken that Sunday, so my surgery was put off until Monday at 11:30 a.m. I lay in the hospital from 10:30 a.m. Sunday until 11:30 a.m. on Monday, totaling 25 hours before surgery. The amazing thing was that I took no pain shots or pain pills. I told them to wrap me in warm blankets and hopefully I would be all right, so that is what they did.

My husband and my grandson were notified and drove the 115 miles to the hospital that night to spend it with me in my room. Sleep was impossible; I was too miserable. It was a long night!

My doctor and nurses said that I had broken all records. They stated that before me, no one hospitalized with a broken hip had refused pain shots. They found that my willpower was very strong. I told them I found that complaining did not help.

In my past I have endured more pain than most anyone has ever experienced. I had tolerated pain before I learned that God had given me power over pain. Since then, I have found that I have power over pain and that pain is an evil tormenting spirit sent from satan. Now I can make pain leave in Jesus' Name. In Luke 10:19 Jesus gave us power over all the enemy's power. That includes both sickness or pain. A spirit of pain will bow and leave if we really get tough and demand it to go, in Jesus' Name!

However, in an emergency situation, another person must rebuke that pain. On that day I had no one with knowledge on the authority that we have to rebuke pain. Yet I refused all pain medication before or after surgery. Three steel pins secured and mended my hip together in surgery the next day. My surgeon said my bones were strong so he foresaw no problems.

Before I had surgery, I told the doctor and nurses that I once had lupus. They did not believe that. They disputed, saying that I never had lupus, as there was no cure for lupus.

They ran lots of blood tests and did an electrocardiogram to be cautious before performing surgery. They found nothing wrong with my health at all. They only found the broken hip socket. They said I was the healthiest person they had seen in the hospital in a long time. I told them that they would not have seen me at all if it were not for that horrible accident.

Surgery was performed on Monday. I left the hospital on Wednesday thinking my home would be like Heaven over the hospital! I was pleased to get a good report from my tests, but ready to go home. I left the hospital with no instructions other than to contact a doctor near me to have my staples removed in ten days. I rode 115 miles home on large cushions, lying down in the back of my Honda Accord station wagon.

My new doctor showed little interest in my case because he had not performed my surgery. He never discovered that the steel pins in my hip had slipped out of place until more than one month later. Then, since my pain had intensified, he took another x-ray. It showed that the bones were not connecting, so my hip was not healing. I stayed in bed for another month without any physical therapy. Satan was determined to keep me off my computer. He really tried to stop me from completing this book.

I informed satan that he was not wise by making his last attack. Each time that he attacks, I get a stronger anointing in that area in which he attacks. That makes him a loser as now I have a strong anointing for bones and backs. I hate the devil. By God's help satan cannot stop me from doing what God called me to do. Satan was only able to delay me. However, I came back stronger and more determined than ever to resist his evil deeds.

My accident stopped some speaking engagements and cancelled two airline flights. But I was blessed to be home with time to pray and get closer to God. I spent time on the phone praying for those whom satan had attacked. I prayed for some cancer victims, and I got the pain spirits off everyone calling me who had been attacked. Satan's evil pain spirits bowed, as I prayed in Jesus' Name, as I lay there mending my broken hip.

It is now August, three months since my hip was broken. I am doing well and I am on my computer finishing my book. Satan cannot stop my book nor can he stop me until God is finished with my work. I am a strong-willed person whose mind is made up to finish what God called me to do. I will not quit until after the work that God called me to do is completed here on earth!

My spirit and my determination is stronger than ever, to spoil or stop satan's evil plans. Soon I will be traveling and ministering for the Lord once again. With God's help, my postponed speaking engagements will soon all be filled.

God knew that I needed to pull aside for three months to rest and be refreshed. I was so busy that I had no time for myself, my children, or my three grandsons. One grandson said that he had to get an appointment to speak to me! That is too busy! I never had the heart to turn hurting people away.

I realize now that being too busy is another one of satan's tricks. If he cannot stop our ministry, then he will push as hard as he can until we spend more time with people than we spend with God. I know for certain that is not God's will!

If satan is able to get us too busy praying for those calling for prayer, then he may get us too busy to pray for our family or ourselves. It is best to shut off the phone sometimes and spend time away from people who may steal our quality time from the Lord and family. I know I must adjust my future schedules because Jesus and my family are both important to me.

I rejoice and praise the Lord that He has kept me protected through satan's evil attacks for so many years. Satan has tried to destroy me from my infancy. My angels must surely stay busy watching over and protecting me. (See Psalms 34:7.) "Many are the afflictions of the righteous, but the Lord delivers him out of them all." (Psalms 34:19). Praise God He has never failed me!

I am healed from all of satan's many attacks! And God continually renews my strength as an eagle. I praise Him for the power of His Word that turned my life away from defeat and brought victory to me through speaking God's Holy Word! Amen!

Chapter 17

Emily's Poems and Guidance Scriptures

"Satan Is a Bluff"

Satan bluffs us—we see, as Jesus prayed for me,
By applying God's Word as truth has set me free,
I am Spirit-filled, and now I am shouting for glee!

Beware of satan fooling you; he once fooled me,
So you enforce God's Word, and it sets you free.
Do heed my warning plea, as victory you'll see!

Though satan may be prince or power of the air,
Don't fear him; we abide within God's good care,
Let satan roar, as God saves us with His power!

God is our refuge; He is a mighty strong tower,
So let's worship Him and throw off every care,
In God's presence no other love can compare!

While I'm trusting Jesus I have His good favor,
So I am salt on earth, He's my Lord and Savior,
Jesus abides within me, now together we labor!

God's Word redeemed me from satan's scam,
So, I am shouting, oh glory to God, truly I am,
Eternally free, I am redeemed by God's Lamb!

By wisdom I did not meditate satan's fables,
I whipped deception, and Jesus made me able,
Since I am Holy Spirit filled—I remain stable!

I meditated the Word; Jesus' Blood I did plea,
Satan had intended that I must never go free!
Good-bye lupus—1983, as death I did not see!

The lupus battle took me twelve months' time,
My battle was fierce in both body and mind,
I won the lupus battle, as truth became mine!

I ran to Jesus and climbed out of a lupus trap,
Now in my book I teach you how to climb out,
You enforce God's Word, and then climb out!

God gave my poems as I taught at Dr. Hayes's healing school in 1996.

"In Jesus We Safely Abide"

We are free from the sin curse, from sickness or shame,
And we were freed by the power in Jesus' Holy name.
He washed us in His Word; we cannot stay the same.

His power keeps us moment by moment, hour by hour.
Within God's grace I partake of His anointed power.
By stating the Word in prayer did give Satan a big scare!

I quoted God's Word and the Word made a big impact,
The Word brought me back as I wasn't lazy or slack,
As Jesus paid my ransom by the stripes on His back.

Now I'm safe within Jesus—without sin or its shame,
Satan lied; I escaped his death trap, which is plain!
Luke 10:19 is no game; satan's crippled; he is lame!

I abide in God's blessings; Jesus made the exchange.
Though satan half killed me, ignorance was to blame.
But now, satan cannot destroy me as my tongue I tame!

The more satan tries me, the closer to Jesus I abide,
Satan's trials will only purify me if in Jesus I will hide.
His Word is a road map, while His Spirit is my guide!

"A Godly Mother Prays"

Our godly mother will win the heart of her Heavenly Father,
Though she loves her family she places God above all other,
Children gather around and call her their wonderful mother.

She will cook the meals and see that the family is well fed,
Then read the Bible to children before tucking them in bed.
A godly mother prays and talks to God over each sleepy head.

She then cleans house and washes her family's dirty clothes.
Mother bestows kindness and wipes her children's runny nose.
She is the glue that connects a family; she is one God chose.

She works diligently until long past the setting of the sun.
As all in her house are fast asleep her work has only begun.
That godly mother still prays fervently to God for each one.

*Our Master wants us to save our families and
    spare no cost,
You must catch His urgent vision and then pray
    your utmost.
If mother gets too busy to pray her family will all
    be lost!*

*Mother's phone rings requesting urgent prayer to
    our Lord
Someone's child strayed; so two mothers pray in
    one accord
So fervently pray as life without prayer no one can
    afford!*

*As a mother's wayward child did stray in sin's
    dark plight.
That godly mother prays until that child gets
    things right.
At times she prays for her grandchildren through
    the night!*

*Then mother loses her youth; she gets wrinkled,
    then gray.
She will age and pass away—so take roses,
    brighten her day,
Children, never forget how mother's prayers paved
    your way!*

"Our Good Shepherd"

We live without fear as our shepherd abides within,
His kindness is everlasting; His love knows no end,
Jesus is my Good Shepherd, on Him I can depend!

When my heart is so heavy, I find peace and
* calm,*
My Bible says God engraved my name in His
* Palm,*
The battle can end by devouring God's 23rd
* Psalm!*

"Our Daily Prayer"

From on top of my head to the sole of my feet,
I rest in God's power and from satan's defeat,
By God's Spirit I'm happy and in Him complete!

Lord, we pray for Divine wisdom now for today,
Help me shine a light on my brother's pathway,
Help me to say things that I want him to say!

As I forgive others, Lord, so forgive also me,
Temper my words and deeds with love I plea,
Lord give me wisdom as I surrender unto Thee!

Keep me from sickness, accidents, and from sin,
Now teach me to be patient and kind to all men,
Lord, give me peace and put new courage within.

I pray for a new vision and strength for today,
Lord, thanks for life and for more love I pray,
Then I can lift others that fall by life's way.

Thanks for my home, food, raiment and joy within,
I am grateful to Jesus as He died for all my sin,
For my renewed life, Jesus on you I depend;
  Amen!

Every obstacle and situation in life can be victoriously overcome and turned into victory, as we partake of the Divine nature of God provided through the cross of Jesus Christ.

As believers, our lives include both valleys and mountains. None are excluded from satan's attack. "Many are the afflictions of the righteous, but the Lord delivers him out of them all" (Ps. 34:19). We may endure attacks tonight, but joy will come when the sun shines in the morning if we stay focused on God.

Our Victory Confession

Confess this page daily. Say: "By Jesus' stripes according to Isaiah 53:5 and First Peter 2:24 I am healed. God's Word is true and satan's report is a lie! I do not waver or doubt God's promises; they are true and they are for me. I will faithfully call Jesus my healer and miracle worker every day of my life.

"Jesus is my High Priest and I confess that no cancer demon, lupus demon, or, (insert your diagnosis)_____ will kill me. I enforce Luke 10:19. Jesus has redeemed and set me free from all curses. I put all satan's sickness curses underneath my feet. I enforce God's Word and hold His Word above all satan's attacks, and I will get victory over all circumstances!

"My body is the temple of the Holy Spirit. I am kept by God's power because I surrender my will to His will. Satan has no right to keep me sick. Jesus took stripes on His back so I could be healed. I claim those stripes for my body in Jesus' Name. Jesus paid the price for my healing. I will not allow satan to steal it away. I tread my enemy under my feet as Jesus said for us to do in Luke 10:19. I will win my faith battle!"

"I will overcome this evil attack by the Blood of the Lamb and by the words of my testimony. My testimony is the truth of God's Word. I will take charge of my thoughts and bring them under subjection to God's Word. I agree with God's Word and I apply the Word to my body for my healing in Jesus' Name! Amen!"

Guidance Scriptures on Various Subjects

ADDICTION	Gal. 5:1; Jn. 8:32; Prov. 20:1
AGING	Prov. 9:11; Eccles. 11:10; Prov. 10:27
ANGER	1 Pet. 2:23; Eph. 4:26-27; 1 Thess. 5:9
ANXIETY	Jn. 14:27; Phil. 4:6-8; Ps. 46:1-3

BEREAVEMENT	1 Cor. 15:54-57; Is. 25:8; 1 Thess. 4:13-14
BITTERNESS	Eph. 4:31; Heb. 12:15; Jas. 3:14-15
CARNALITY	Rom. 6:6-9; Eph. 4:22-24; 2 Cor. 4:16
CONDEMNATION	Rom. 8:1; Rom. 3:10-12; Is. 64:6-8
CONFUSION	Is. 26:3; 1 Cor. 14:33; Is. 55:8-9
DEATH	Rom. 14:7-8; Job 19:26-27; Is. 25:8
DEPRESSION	Neh. 8:10; Phil. 4:8; Rom. 8:28
DISSATISFACTION	Prov. 27:20; Heb. 13:5-6; 1 Tim. 6:6-8
DOUBT	Jas. 4:8; Rom. 10:17; Heb. 10:32,35,39
FAILURE	Prov. 24:16-18; Ps. 145:14-16; 2 Cor. 3:5
FEAR	2 Tim. 1:7; Phil. 4:13; Rev. 1:17-18
FINANCES	Mt. 6:31-34; Ps. 37:25-26; Phil. 4:19
ILLNESS	Jas. 5:14; Ps. 37:25-26; Phil. 4:19
INSECURITY	2 Thess. 3:3; Ps. 91:3-7; 2 Cor.3:4-5
JUDGING	1 Cor. 4:5; Mt. 7:3-5; Jn. 5:22
LONELINESS	Jn. 14:18; Ps. 147:3; Ps. 27:10
LUST	2 Pet. 2:9; Mt. 18:8-9; Prov. 6:25-26
MARRIAGE	2 Cor. 6:14-17; 1 Cor. 7:10-17; Heb. 13:4
PRIDE	Mt. 18:2-4; Prov. 27:1-2; Lk. 18:11-14
SATAN	Eph. 6:10-17; 1 Jn. 4:1-3; Lk. 10:18-19

SUFFERING	Heb. 5:8-9; 2 Cor. 4:8-10; 1 Pet. 4:19
TEMPTATION	Jas. 1:12; 2 Pet. 2:9; Jas. 1:2-4
TRIALS	2 Tim. 2:3; 1 Pet. 4:12-13; Ps. 34:17
WEAKNESS	2 Cor. 12:9; 1 Jn. 5:5; I Jn. 2:15-17

May God bless you today!

To order books, cassette tapes, or to book speaking engagements, you may write to the following address:

Emily C. Dotson
1196 Hillview Drive
King, NC. 27021-9709

Only money orders or cashier's checks are accepted for tape or book orders!

If ordering a price list, send a stamped addressed envelope with one dollar to cover postage cost. Then I will know that you are serious about ordering! Thanks! In Jesus, Emily C. Dotson.

Please make a decision today to stand on God's Word for salvation or for healing! Document your agreement with God's Word. Fill in the blanks with your decision, and mail me a copy.

Your name_____Day_____
Date_____Time_____
Decision:_____-

_____
_____
_____
_____
_____
_____
_____
_____